Postcolonial Interruptions,
Unauthorised Modernities

Radical Cultural Studies

Series Editors:
Fay Brauer, Maggie Humm, Tim Lawrence, Stephen Maddison,
Ashwani Sharma and Debra Benita Shaw
(Centre for Cultural Studies Research, University of East London, UK)

The *Radical Cultural Studies* series publishes monographs and edited collections to provide new and radical analyses of the culturopolitics, sociopolitics, aesthetics and ethics of contemporary cultures. The series is designed to stimulate debates across and within disciplines, foster new approaches to Cultural Studies and assess the radical potential of key ideas and theories.

Titles in the Series

Sewing, Fighting and Writing: Radical Practices in Work, Politics and Culture, by Maria Tamboukou
Radical Space: Exploring Politics and Practice, edited by Debra Benita Shaw and Maggie Humm
Science Fiction, Fantasy and Politics: Transmedia World-Building Beyond Capitalism, by Dan Hassler-Forest
EU, Europe Unfinished: Europe and the Balkans in a Time of Crisis, edited by Zlatan Krajina and Nebojša Blanuša
Postcolonial Interruptions, Unauthorised Modernities, by Iain Chambers
Austerity as Public Mood: Social Anxieties and Social Struggles, by Kirsten Forkert (forthcoming)
Metamodernism: Historicity, Affect, Depth, edited by Robin van den Akker, Alison Gibbons and Timotheus Vermeulen (forthcoming)
Pornography, Materiality and Cultural Politics, by Stephen Maddison (forthcoming)

Postcolonial Interruptions, Unauthorised Modernities

Iain Chambers

ROWMAN &
LITTLEFIELD
———INTERNATIONAL———
London • New York

Published by Rowman & Littlefield International, Ltd.
Unit A, Whitacre Mews, 26-34 Stannary Street, London SE11 4AB
www.rowmaninternational.com

Rowman & Littlefield International, Ltd. is an affiliate of Rowman & Littlefield
4501 Forbes Boulevard, Suite 200, Lanham, Maryland 20706, USA
With additional offices in Boulder, New York, Toronto (Canada), and London (UK)
www.rowman.com

Copyright © 2017 by Iain Chambers

All rights reserved. No part of this book may be reproduced in any form or by any electronic or mechanical means, including information storage and retrieval systems, without written permission from the publisher, except by a reviewer who may quote passages in a review.

British Library Cataloguing in Publication Information Available
A catalogue record for this book is available from the British Library

ISBN: HB 978-1-7866-0331-9
ISBN: PB 978-1-7866-0332-6

Library of Congress Cataloging-in-Publication Data

Library of Congress Cataloging-in-Publication Data Available

978-1-78660-331-9 (cloth : alk. paper)
978-1-78660-332-6 (pbk. : alk. paper)
978-1-78660-333-3 (electronic)

∞™ The paper used in this publication meets the minimum requirements of American National Standard for Information Sciences Permanence of Paper for Printed Library Materials, ANSI/NISO Z39.48-1992.

Printed in the United States of America

Contents

Acknowledgements		vii
1	The Algebra of Power	1
2	A Broken Archive	17
3	Migrating Modernities	37
4	Lessons from the South	61
5	Scarred Landscapes	83
6	Folds in Time	101
Bibliography		129
Index		139

Acknowledgements

I wish to thank Gennaro Postiglione from Milan Polytechnic for initially sucking me into a project on the European museum—MeLa (http://www.mela-project.polimi.it). This allowed me, together with colleagues in Naples—Lidia Curti, Alessandra De Angelis, Beatrice Ferrara, Giulia Grechi, Celeste Ianniciello, Mariangela Orabona, Michaela Quadraro—to explore the critical impact of modern migration on the premises and practices of the contemporary museum.

Students at the University Orientale of Naples were a constant factor in my readings and research. With them I explored nearly all of the issues presented here, along with other students in the PhD program in Cultural and Postcolonial Studies and its present resurgence within the more extensive curriculum of International Studies. A further, and more experimental, critical laboratory has also been consistently provided in the lengthy seminars and talks at the Centre for Postcolonial and Gender Studies, also at the Orientale.

For comments and exchanges, as well as for providing intellectual stimulus and debate I thank Silvana Carotenuto, Miguel Mellino, Tiziana Terranova, Marina Vitale, Sandro Mezzadra, Mara De Chiara, Gennaro Ascione, and all those who in recent years have invited me to give talks and have critically engaged with what I have had to say. Isaac Julien, Mark Nash, Jimmie Durham, and Marie Thereza Alves encouraged me through their artistic practices and critical example. I also want to thank Luca Guadagnino for inviting me to partecipate in his film on Italian colonialism, *Inconscio Italiano* (2011), and Giacomo Sferlazzo for inducing me to give a talk on music and migration under the midday sun amongst bemused bathers on a Lampedusa beach.

Finally, thanks to Stuart Hall, who first opened the door for me on this critical and political journey more than forty years ago, and to Lidia, who then took me elsewhere, deepened it all, and has continued to accompany me along the way.

Some of the arguments present in this book have initially been aired in diverse publications and places. I began exploring some of the perspectives developed in chapter 2 in 'Cultural and Postcolonial Studies', published in Rosi Braidotti, ed., *After Postructuralism: Transitions and Transformations* (2013). Certain themes in chapter 3 were developed in the precise context of the Italian southern question in 'The Southern Question . . . Again', in Andrea Mammone, Ercole Giap Parini and Giuseppe A. Veltri, eds., *The Routledge Handbook of Contemporary Italy* (2015). Several of the arguments assembled in chapter 5 were first rehearsed in 'Space, Memory, Rhythm, and Time. Constructing a Mediterranean Archive', *New Geographies 05: The Mediterranean* (Harvard Graduate School of Design, 2013), and 'Heterotopia and the Critical Cut', in Mariangela Palladino and John Miller, eds., *The Globalization of Space* (2015). All of this material has been radically reworked into the present remix, hopefully suggesting further connections and a fresh critical cut.

Chapter One

The Algebra of Power

Returning recently to the beautifully woven text and images of John Berger and Jean Mohr's prescient work on migration, *A Seventh Man*, published some forty odd years ago, I came across this significant judgement:

> History, political theory, sociology can help one to understand that 'the normal' is only normative. Unfortunately these disciplines are usually used to do the opposite: to serve tradition by asking questions in such a way that the answers sanctify the norms as absolutes.[1]

I feel this is the case, and even more so today. The contemporary organisation of awareness and knowledge overwhelmingly serves to establish an uninterrupted language of conformity. It leads to structural change being obfuscated. Interrogation is silenced in a consensus that refuses to consider our language, position and the making of meaning. Disagreement and disturbance, and not the procedures that seek to crush them, are merely considered 'ideological'. Whatever troubles the status quo is rapidly labelled an anomaly or deviancy: transitory instances of local emergencies on the flat plateau of agreed procedures.

Opposed to this critical foreclosure, I would like to suggest that contemporary migration, or the racism that precedes and accompanies it, is precisely not, as we are taught to believe, about a set of exceptions or emergencies. Both are woven deeply into the web of Western democracy, into its historical and cultural life. With death spilling out of the headlines—from drownings in the Mediterranean to racial shootings in America's inner cities, the violent surveillance of territories and lives in Palestine, bomb attacks and mass shootings in European capitals—I would also argue that the limits and hypocrisies of the moral economy of the Occident are being continually exposed. The enemy—invariably non-European, non-white, and non-Christian, fundamentally 'queer' with respect to the normative—is immediately identified and externalised. These are the limits of a precise history and its structures of power. They speak of the critical and political responsibilities for those processes that have brought us to where we are today. This pushes us to understand the present movement of migration from the multiple souths of the planet, the consistency of racism and the rendering of certain ethnic groups, minorities and associated cultures as second class citizens or not yet modern, as a historical condition. These are not temporary phenomena or accidental pathologies; they involve structured, historical processes and apparatuses of power. Insisting that such questions are central, and not peripheral, to modernity is not simply of economical, sociological or anthropological importance. What we touch here are the very mechanisms of knowledge and power that legitimate the present order.

MODERNITY AS HEGEMONY

It is also here that we are forced increasingly to recognise that the democracy inherited from the liberal state—now fundamentally blocked in the abstract grammar of eighteenth-century constitutionalism and caricatured in the superficial sensationalisms of the mass media—is increasingly gutted and reduced to the state of oligarchy. An accentuated individualism, legally extended and secured in private property rights, increasingly cancels social space and public responsibilities. The accentuated utilitarianism of neoliberalism and the absolute valorisation of the individual today produces an immanent order in which there are apparently no longer external relations and forces. As Margaret Thatcher succinctly summed it up in 1987: 'There is no such thing as society'. Everything is now domesticated and individualised as the factor of life itself. Here the historical antagonism between the prospects of democracy and individual self-realisation have slipped far beyond their earlier and more restricted confines. Ideas connected to the fair distribution of resources and opportunities have been crushed by the ideological triumph of responsibilities that serve only to confirm the individual. The autonomy of the self now reaches into the sinews of public government: policing and security, like health and education, are not only atomised in response to restricted individual access and personal wealth, they also become autonomous agencies, increasingly only answerable to their budgets, agendas and language. If the United States today is the most blatant example, it is not alone. As in so many areas of modern life, it sets the trend for a wave washing through the West and the world.

The presumptions that surround and sustain such concepts as the 'individual', 'citizenship', 'democracy' and 'freedom' are themselves the products of such mechanisms. While they continue to be presented as neutral and abstract ideals, their practices tell us a very different story. What has been repressed in the representation points us to other maps and temporalities in a planetary modernity that is not merely 'ours' to define. If the politics of explaining and managing the modern world can only be sustained though the violent maintenance of unequal relations of power and the associated negation of other voices and histories, then perhaps we should ask ourselves what precisely does this universality, its democracy and modernity, consist of? This is to entertain seriously the idea that modernity itself is historically and culturally the precise mode of Occidental hegemony and that we need therefore to confront and unpack its premises and practices. At the same time, this modernity cannot simply be cast aside or cancelled. It is, after all, the matrix in which we all move, are positioned, and work to find ourselves and other promises and prospects.

COLONIAL FALL-OUT

It is this rough, undone and frayed web that sustains the arguments in this book. Their gestation occurs very much in a European ambient. There exists no pretence to explain or speak in the name of the non-Occidental world. Here, where my words deliberately fall short, the presumed distinctions between the West and the rest, centre and periphery, are rather problematised and exposed. Altogether more fluid geographies and transitory territories now encroach upon inherited understandings and views. Hierarchies of power and command are increasingly multiple and heterogeneous. This is to begin to register the limits of a knowledge formation that operates as though it were the unique global paradigm, whose history is History *tout court*. So, to insist on gaps in the account means to listen to other accents and rhythms, to register resonance and dissonance. This is deliberately to disband the particular form of historical reasoning that secures Occidental thought and practices in a theology of 'progress' and its linear conquest of space and time. In a word, it is to slip away from the colonial imperatives that made the West the West. Here, in the break-up of European historicism—where only the West is warranted to tell the tale—the subterranean tempos of deeper times and longer rhythms are rendered proximate. The colonial past, conquests, racist slavery and the division of the world among imperial powers are never simply 'back there'; they are constitutive of the present. They live on and continue to mould our comprehension of the existing world. This situation urgently implies changing the conditions of knowledge and posing the 'problem of writing critical histories of the postcolonial present'.[2]

Engaged with the mixing and mutation of time and space, other cultures and lives translate our coordinates from the presumed stability that reflects *our* passage into a heterogeneous scene seeding different histories and multiple trajectories. The world is crossed and cut-up. It is folded into diverse narratives that refuse to be blocked in a uniform accounting of time. It is precisely in this sense that contemporary migration and racism open an archive; an archive that is not so much an institution as a site of ongoing historical processes and the location of continuing social and political antagonisms. Here colonialism, migration and racism can no longer be contained in the categories of economical or sociological phenomena. Rather, they become instances of epistemological and ontological inquiry. As structures of historical violence they challenge the placid presumptions of both our knowledge and our everyday lives. They produce a modernity incorporated and imagined by other bodies and histories; in particular, by the so-called non-Western world which in being 'worlded' by the Occidental turns out to be both *internal* and central to the West that considers itself to be the unique measure of the planet.

> The Industrial Revolution, misleadingly figuring in popular consciousness as an autochthonous metropolitan phenomenon, required colonial land and labour to produce its raw materials just as centrally as it required metropolitan factories and an industrial proletariat to process them, whereupon the colonies were again required as a market. The expropriated Aboriginal, enslaved African American, or indentured Asian is as thoroughly modern as the factory worker, bureaucrat, or *flâneur* of the metropolitan centre.[3]

Such intimacies are directly distilled in the intricate relationships of the formation of the modern European nation state, its cultures, cities, and its unilateral fashioning of the world where modernity, colonialism and capitalism became one. This is not about adding the equations of culture and power to the economic formula. It is about an altogether more complex coming together in a precise political economy. Here, to extend the map of the modern nation and include the colonial spaces over which it exercised its military, political and economic authority, is to change our very understanding of what constitutes the contemporary polity, its wealth, culture and population.[4] This is to chart its making and practices on a very different map where the colonial periphery turns out to be integral to the making of metropolitan life and culture. Genocide, massacres and all the brutal violence of colonial appropriation and territorial aggression come now to be registered within the making of the modern European nation state. They are not unfortunate incidents, terrible tragedies, taking place far from home. They are constitutive of home itself.

CRUEL COMBINATIONS

This leads to unwinding the claims of democracy and citizenship, of rights and the rule of law, in an altogether more extensive and unauthorised space. For if European states sought to establish their authority in the singularity of the nation, their rivalry remains persistently colonial in continuing to contest the spoils of the planet. Decolonialising this inheritance does not merely mean finally to pay attention to the so-called colonial periphery of yesterday, recovering its histories and registering injustice. Bomb attacks, mass shootings and civilian deaths in Madrid, London, Paris and Bruxelles, render dramatically proximate similar events in Tunis, Beirut, Baghdad, Kabul, Lahore and Peshawar. Here the colonial concoctions that configured modernity (the European carve-up of Africa and the invention of the 'Middle East') take their revenge on the present. In more immediate terms, raging continual warfare on Muslim countries for almost three decades, from Iraq to Afghanistan, Libya and Syria, leading to the death of more than 500,000 civilians, inevitably leads to what political commentators call blowback. As the writer Hanif Kureishi put it in the aftermath of the London bombings of 2005: 'Modern Western politicians believe we can murder real others in faraway places without the same thing happening to us, and without any physical or moral suffering on our part'.[5] This is to forcibly remind ourselves of the cruel combinations of colonial histories and postcolonial proximities that come to be stitched into the very fabric of the modern metropolis. Pulled through these examples into a deeper historical trough we confront the brutal evidence of Occidental colonialism being involved in a perpetual war on the rest of the planet for the last five centuries.

> When Europeans arrived in what is now Latin America in 1492, the region may have been inhabited by between 50 million and 100 million indigenous people. By the mid 1600s, their population was slashed to about 3.5 million. The vast majority succumbed to foreign disease and many were slaughtered, died of slavery or starved to death after being kicked off their land. It was like the holocaust seven times over.[6]

Tzevtan Todorov has referred to this history as humanity's greatest genocide.[7]

It is in this precise sense that the urgency of a postcolonial perspective is not simply about rescuing forgotten histories and denied lives, and finally adding them to the previous account. The other voices and visions that arrive from the so-called margins of modernity, once directly colonised, today bracketed in the categories of the developing and underdeveloped world, promote a sharp epistemological challenge. The very premises of a modernity no longer guaranteed by a unique universalism is disrupted and dispersed. The exercise of scientific neutrality and critical distance fall apart in a worldly space in which power, no matter how complex, multifaceted and subtle its exercise, exposes a geopolitical provenance, a series of cultural agendas, a historical will; that is, a series, intricate and unintended, of hegemonies at work. It is precisely through this heterogeneous complexity, even when exposed in scholarly subtleties and sensitive attention to detail, that hegemony, as opposed to mere instrumental domination, is reproduced. Its manner of narration, no matter how liberal or 'multicultural' it may seek to be, structurally excludes whatever seeks to challenge its manner of recognising itself and registering others. This, is what the Peruvian anthropologist Anibal Quijano calls the coloniality of power rendered as knowledge.[8] The methodology legitimates the dominion of the discourse. What I will be arguing here, against that dominion, is that the pieces of an increasingly fragmented tradition can no longer be put back together again. They now constitute a broken archive. Historically inherited elements can only be reassembled in an ongoing configuration where the old binaries of south and north fall away to be replaced by an altogether more heterogeneous and overlapping set of relations. When the once excluded and elsewhere is also in here, then the proximities of dissonance and resonance within an increasing conviviality of languages and localities touches the complexities of all the components.

So, the break-up of empire is not about its immediate cancellation; the colonial inheritance cannot simply be wiped off the slate. It is rather about the emerging assemblage of what has been subordinated or simply excluded from the existing framing and explanation of modernity. This implies engaging with spaces and practices that propose other rhythms and reasons. In the present circumstances these may well be negated, subordinated and reduced to marginal cultures and local histories, unable to claim the universal validity of the West. Nevertheless they exist, persist and resist within that very same modernity as a sore, a wound, a persistent interrogation; what the anthropologist Tarek Elhaik refers us to as an 'incurable image'.[9] These are the other histories, and not exclusively human, that ghost our present. They hold Occidental modernity up to the light, exposing its shadows. They propose a re-membering of the world that evokes other manners of narrating, other shapes and figures that support understandings of the past-present-future. The archive slips beyond unique control. Modes of classification and meaning multiply. Worldly coordinates loom into view and another universalism begins to emerge: one not dictated and scripted solely by us.

EXCEEDING THE FRAME

Recognising the irreducibility of the world to a single frame or explanation clearly raises awkward questions that disturb the universal premises of the human and social sciences. The historical awareness of the contingent configuration of knowledge formations as spatial processes and combinatory constellations is accompanied by the disbanding of a unique understanding of time. Despite its global grip, the supersession and subsequent synthesis that apparently leads from one chronological moment to another, charted along a sequential linearity called 'progress', turns out to be a regional and provincial topos. This leads to understanding that subaltern and subordinated elements do not simply constitute a potential counter-hegemony in the dialectic of historical becoming and political understanding. Rather, as heterogeneous fragments and practices they continually threaten to interrupt and undo the hegemonic drive and desire for a unique telling and framing of the world. They are heterotopic; that is they already here among us, they co-exist, they are contemporary. Although they cannot replace hegemony with a complete or utopian alternative, they can transform and rework its rationality through other forms of reasoning. Undoing the premises of a particular social and political order is not to cancel that history and heritage, as if that were possible; rather, it is to reassemble the refuse of that broken archive into another set of perspectives and possibilities.

This unfolding critical space is not restricted to being exposed in a generalised critique of Occidental hegemony. It can also be tracked in the very language and grammar of knowledge production and its associated 'scholarship'. For all of its subtleties and sophistications, and even in its most critical mode, the latter overwhelmingly clings to modalities of argument disciplined by the unquestioned sequentiality of language and illusions of transparency. Here scholarship is often simply the synonym for academic liberalism and the unquestioned archive upon which it draws in elaborating understandings of balance, distance and neutrality. Scholarship itself, evoking the combination of institutional support, financing and erudition, is, of course, deeply ambiguous when considered in terms of political and cultural hegemony. Clearly there is no simple exit from this linguistic, institutional and semantic bind. Still, to register and work these limits into the critical language deployed is already to breach a structure of sense that is so powerfully endorsed in practices—from university syllabuses to peer-reviewed journals, competitive university rankings, impact factors and uniform style sheets—that sustain and reproduce this limited logic as the unique measure of truth. In another context—that of the contemporary Muslim world—subservience to this logic has been bluntly identified as 'intellectual slavery', and is considered to be the continuation of a colonising tradition.[10] Opposed to scholarship seeking to nail meaning and hang it out to dry under the sun of a purported science, there remains the challenge of a language that 'relocates its relation to truth within historicity, and not against it'.[11]

To contest such a situation is not to suggest a simple revocation, rather it is to consider the redistribution of resources and knowledge in a fashion that exceeds their reproduction and disciplining as a mirror of the existing state of affairs. To draw upon an earlier lexicon, this is to puncture the pretensions of education and research as an ideological state apparatus or ISA. Obviously, our understandings of knowledge, the state and ideology have shifted sharply since Louis Althusser's noted essay on the question. However, like an indelible stain, the pertinence of such arguments, which reach back to Antonio Gramsci and his insistence on the centrality of culture in the production and reproduction of political hegemony and power (where the distinction between politics and culture increasingly falls away), survives and lives on to disturb our present.

Turning to other languages for critical and historical understanding also implies seeding doubt in the procedures and premises of those disciplinary accounts of modernity that promised, via the rarely considered positivism and historicism of their nineteenth-century incubation, to render the world transparent to our will. This is what, more than half a century ago, Horkheimer and Adorno referenced as the 'world of the administered life' that leads to the 'conversion of enlightenment into positivism'.[12] As Gramsci insisted in the *Prison Notebooks*, it is precisely such positivism that promotes the critical and political passivity that sustains the status quo. It is not by chance that today the purported neutrality of the social 'sciences' is increasingly making a historical rendezvous with the equally universal claims of a unilateral neoliberalism and its particular 'public pedagogy'.[13] Both believe—as though there were a 'historical activity outside history' — that the world can be fully audited, researched and resourced, and knowledge rendered fully translatable to the algorithms of information.[14] It leads to dispossession and privatisation. Education as a public good is replaced by learning as an investment in cognitive capital.[15] There is apparently no alternative to the existing political economy of knowledge... and power. To insist on a critical interrogation of this state of affairs is precisely to disseminate disturbance and disorder. For a critical citizenship can hardly avoid seeing and living the political paradoxes between culture and capital, between science, technology, power and declarations of neutrality, between pedagogy and the public performance of a diminishing democracy now shackled to the brutal pragmatics of capitalist governance. Critical knowledge becomes a problem, even a subversive activity.[16] For to think clearly on these points, as Aimé Césaire pointed out many decades ago, is to think dangerously.[17]

All of this brings us to consider how academic scholarship, its production and custody of knowledge, is not necessarily the only legitimate mode of critically understanding the contemporary world. There are other languages out there—visual and auditory—probing the same space while also producing others. In the final chapter of this book, reasoning with sounds, with music, I suggest that we perhaps need to relax the existing grip on what passes for knowledge (and truth). When language manoeuvres in the dark, refuses to rationalise and insists on the meaning of its meandering, then a gap is installed. Academic reticence, and the reluctance to register its own limits and border zones, invariably evades confronting the intellectual *domus* and epistemological *doxa* that guarantees the recognition and ultimate authority of its own enunciations.[18] The importance of registering the overdetermination of scholarly and academic protocols, and their bordering effects in disciplining and authorising what is, and is not, considered a legitimate discussion, drives the interplay of knowledge and power into another space. Responding to the cracks and leaks in the academic machine is to appreciate how the categories deeply sedimented in its constitution, such as the 'individual', the 'subject', the 'political', or the disciplinary premises of its sociology and history, frequently remain outside the critical conversation. These assemblages directly participate, whether consciously or not, in the idea that the rest of the world can only really come into existence once Occidental categories have been activated. Yet those very same categories are today being traversed by histories, cultures and voices that they previously neither considered nor contemplated. Something is amiss.

The intention here is certainly not to cancel this complex inheritance, rather to re-cast it on a terrain that exceeds its initial provenance and governance. For those in Africa, Asia and the Middle East confronting the European-derived academic machine, its linguistic and cultural limits profoundly signal the epistemological deafness of the European ear. Insisting on such restrictions can generate further understandings that direct us towards other rationalities and diverse knowledge formations. We may have little choice but to work within and across this inherited tradition and hegemony. But this means to work through it, transforming and translating inherited fields and competences into altogether more problematic and porous practices, insisting on inconclusive processes rather than epistemological and institutional verities. To repeat: this is not simply about contesting the present scholarly lexicon and academic arrangement. I, too, have learnt much from the work produced there. It is rather to register in its historical formation the limits that suggest that it is not the only modality of knowledge that exists. There are other ways of writing and narrating, other knowledges, that escape the lust of certain languages for certitude. With this in mind we can better understand the necessary distinction between emancipation (apparently granted by the former colonial master and the Occidental knowledge-power apparatus) and freedom. The latter is only attained through escaping from the terms proposed by the powers of the emancipator. Nobody is really waiting to be emancipated, everybody is seeking to be free.

This, to dramatise the point, is about crossing and disrupting a certain set of confines, and learning, in the profoundest manner, from the modern migrant. It involves seeking to understand the political and historical consequences of the continuous configuration of the world the latter is called upon to enact in order to survive and live on. As a modern political subject, her history in becoming ours undoes an earlier historical and cultural settlement. The increasingly aggressive legal framing of migration now seeps into considerations of rights, and contaminates the earlier and seemingly separate juridical definition of the refugee. Facile distinctions between the flight from political turbulence and that from structural poverty are increasingly impossible to sustain.[19] The nominal separation of the two categories is ruthlessly conjoined in a shared refusal to accommodate either: at the end of the day those in movement to secure their lives are on the same boats and beaches, sharing the same camps and holes in the wire. Overwhelmingly produced by the Occidental management of the globe, these unwanted arrivals crack the mould and introduce unknown factors into the equation. They push existing definitions of citizenship out of joint, proposing postcolonial interrogations.[20] Here we confront the colonial archive that rendered both migration and warfare central to its modernity. This forces apart the desired closure exercised in the hegemonic variants of contemporary knowledge and power that seek to render that past truly buried and forgotten. For colonialism is irreducible to a chronological occasion and historical event.[21] Colonialism, as a temporal and spatial structure, continues to promote the processes that sustain the present.

While the intellectual enterprise comes under increasing pressure from the neoliberal mandate demanding it render itself transparent to the market, its own particular debt to the dark matters of a particular order of power and knowledge is also increasingly difficult to refute. If the liberal university and its humanist programme is clearly in ruins it perhaps becomes historically imperative to re-assemble its debris on other grounds, and to begin to explore the critical honesties of a necessary discontinuity. This inaugurates a scenario in which critical knowledge and existing scholarship do not necessarily share a common trajectory or seamlessly fit together. Here the crisis of the university, particularly in the area of the human and social sciences, is today clearly caught between seeking the unconditional autonomy of critical labour or being reduced to certifying instrumental competences that respect the hegemonic languages and logics of the political economy of the present.

UNLEASHING LANGUAGE

So, apart from the critique of the Occidental academic machine succumbing to the illusion of rendering all accountable to an abstract universalism (that quickly succumbs to the planetary laws of the market as the ultimate verification of social truth), I will come to consider the potential intrusion and interruption sustained by music and the visual arts in helping to free existing language and knowledge from their present framing. In promoting a further space, these practices, and most acutely in their postcolonial evaluation, disseminate a critical disturbance. They produce cuts in time where institutional and consequential linearity fails to conclude. Of course, like the academic and research apparatus, they, too, can be rapidly absorbed back into the circuits of capital and the neoliberal politics of immediately insuring the worth of both the artist-provider and the collector-customer through the registration of monetary value. Still, something lives on even within these punishing exchanges. Dismantling the pragmatic imperative for transparent communication and the immediacy of empirical confirmation that sustains a unilateral grasp of the world, such creative practices insist that there are other narratives, other languages and understandings, simply others, that co-exist within the folds of such an imperious logic. Inviting us to think again, to consider further paths across a differentiated modernity, such art reworks, even deserts, the precious confines of the inherited European aesthetic of the beautiful for an altogether more turbulent and disturbing configuration of the senses. Of course, this cut can be ignored, the exposed wound left to fester, or it can simply be reduced to an incidental artistic embellishment distinct from the 'real' world. Still, it insists.

Much of this has to do with the power and politics of the image. Here the practices of representation, both those of the mass media and the arts, provide us with occasion for thought. There has occurred a historical shift in modern art and aesthetics from the text or singular art object, whose interpretation relies on the linearity of a narrative in both its execution and explanation (for example, the novel or film, their source of origin in the author and the artist, and their subsequent authorisation in art history, literary studies and associated publics) to the collage—both visual and acoustic. In the latter case sense is suspended and sustained in the affective instance of the mix. A rigid historicity is dismantled. Time changes from a singular, chronological passage to be dubbed in the remix and the subsequent condensation of the multiple. Such art is not simply relational.[22] Rather, it is overloaded with the aesthetic and ethics of the historical time of an archive that refuses to pass and accumulates as instructive debris in the present. In this sense the truth is there in the image that consistently exceeds the singular point of view. To understand this affirmation is to weave signs, sounds and silences together into multiple conversations able to dub and disturb dominant figures and rhythms. To register the musicality of narrative and memory, their accents and intervals, their cracks and collusions, is to touch the complexity of a layered set of languages and aesthetics as opposed to the presumed clarity of a sharp and a well-defined image or expression. Such a style of remembering is inevitably political, it draws upon a past that is both registered and unregistered. It is distributed in shifting historical and cultural landscapes, sedimented in multiple archives that remain irreducible to an institutional formation, retrieval and capture that is invariably capitalist and colonial.

The historical European avant-garde, responding to the technological reproduction, mobility and mutation of the image in photography and cinema, clearly drew from the colonial 'periphery' for its experiments in form and language. The geography of the canon, as with all colonialisms, was simultaneously extended and inadvertently contaminated. Is this merely a colonial appropriation, a controlled registration of an extra-European world? In another, more subversive, mapping, coordinated by multiple temporalities, it could also be considered to mark the postcolonial ingression, reworking and interruption of the syntax of a single modernity. The languages of the metropole were not only repeated, reworked, relocated and renewed in yesterday's colonial spaces: Latin America, the Caribbean, sub-Saharan Africa, Aboriginal Australia. They have also increasingly encountered local counter-proposals and traditions that translate both internal and external traces into situated immediacies. This is not simply to register a contemporary phenomenon occurring in the audiovisual arts; rather, it is to acknowledge a profound shift in the interpretative apparatus. If the history of art now comes to be renegotiated in another space where the borders of the discipline are crossed and cut up by contemporary urgencies, then history itself (or rather the historiographical operation) is exposed to another manner of telling. It is dragged out of a chronological straight jacket and recombined in a contemporary arrangement that reworks its past, present (and future) significance.[23]

Here, against the abstract, hence universal, reach of thought, the body breaks into the picture. Marked by the constructions of location, gender and race, ethnicity and sexuality, diverse abilities and orientations, this is a body that refuses to stay still and be confined to an allotted slot in the political and cultural regime. It interrogates the present status of knowledge and its purported democratic order. It threatens all appeals to neutrality, critical distance, and the metaphysics of a transcendent truth. The Occidental apparatus that established such categories through the disciplinary protocols of ethnography, anthropology, sociology and political science is unable to contain its matter, its objects, in the sterile cage of scientificity, references and citation indexes. The facts refuse to stick when the violence of the method is contested by those who reject being objectified. Frantz Fanon's famous refusal to negate his humanity in this objectivity—'Look, a Negro!'—draws us to the violent core of a culture in which subordination through patriarchy, race and racism emerges as necessarily a part of the methodology that maintains the hierarchal order of the world.[24] Behind the mask of universalism such a culture refuses to consider the territorial and historical premises that authorises its voice and knowledge. When the abstract, universal subject of the Occident dissolves into incorporated subjectivities and located singularities the claims of a rationality accustomed to rendering the world responsive to only its language and grammar of power inevitably breaks down.

THE CRACKED VOICE

On the edge of this present critical space, with our *stupor mundi* or wonder before a world that does not respect or mirror only us, there begins a journey towards decolonizing methodologies and loosening the binds of disciplinary authority.[25] This leads to registering cuts and intervals in the body of the Occident for whom research is often synonymous with colonialism. It interrogates the very constitution of what passes for knowledge. As a minimum, the existing syntax of understanding, its conceptual lexicon and institutional legitimation, is forced to mark time in a world also composed by other rhythms and the beats of other traditions and translations. It is pressurised into taking an apprenticeship in listening, even cultivating silences that register a gap, an interval, a fracture, in an emerging critical lexicon where we can learn to recognise our limits.

In a recent essay on transdisciplinarity by Antonia Birnbaum, the author deliberately sets Theodor Adorno speaking on the essay form against the machinery of scholarship. She argues that the essayist—and Walter Benjamin is here our greatest European example—is neither a creator nor a scholar, only a critic. With the critic lies a manner of writing that is opposed to a truth guaranteed by disciplinary protocols. The appeal to an eternal veracity sustained by scientificity and the 'absolute idea of reason' that confirms the 'coincidence between social rationality and its supposedly objective character'(Adorno) is shattered.[26] The essay, as opposed to the scholarly paper or monograph, is a heresy, for it works with the breaks, intervals and undoing of discursive rationality. It seeks to 'reinvent its method within the process of understanding itself'.[27] Here it becomes necessary, as Adorno put it, to free 'irritating and dangerous aspects' in order to uncover the 'memory of the non-conceptual knowledge that adheres to the concept'.[28] I suppose, however tentatively, that is what I am trying to achieve in these pages.

The algebra of power that produces accredited universal knowledge and history while discrediting other knowledges as local and indigenous, hence limited, are the powers that form and discipline the world in a manner so that its mental and material coordinates become one. Understandings of 'freedom', 'democracy', 'citizenship', and the liberal language that authorises them, are presumed to have unequivocal definitions. Yet if we are willing to recognise that there are other ways of inhabiting these categories and practices, that they can be grounded in multiple and non-universal conditions, then we need also to recognise that the present economy of knowledge rests on a precise and precarious arrangement of powers.[29] Its universal claims cannot obfuscate its particular historical formation and cultural collocation in the political economy that colonised the world, pursuing the realisation of that particular universalism. Occidental knowledge and practices, too, are caught up in the capitalist relationships of production that have configured modernity. In both institutional and individual terms, they, too, are caught and sustained in the present-day molecularisation of physical and cognitive labour, tracked in digital algorithms that research performance and product, while the ivory towers of learning increasingly crumble into the market place. If those practices and institutions have historically been the harbinger of critical thought, today that possibility is increasingly being shut down in the name of cost efficiency, audit transparency, market evaluation and cultural product. Here critical work is increasingly considered an impediment, marginal grit that threatens the smooth operations of the academic machinery. Here 'the only responsible criticism is the one that does not criticise; the sole objection is the one that is consensual; the only alternative is endorsement'.[30]

This darkening scenario of the cannibalising powers of capitalism seeking to subordinate all to its destructive creativity suggests a critical move that might paradoxically retrieve the Occidental archive and its knowledge formation from that destiny. For, as I have suggested, the arguments presented here are not about annulment. Against a linear understanding of the accumulation of knowledge in which the West seeks to retain its legislative power, other knowledges cannot simply be subordinated or colonised. Rather, in recognising their repressed historical presence *within* the making of modernity we are led into considering reconfigurations that propose another critical constellation. If this means to break open the archive that continues to catalogue the privileged history of the Occident (even when it is talking about others and the elsewhere), it means also to embark on journeys into far wider critical spaces. There authority will have to be renegotiated, decomposed and recomposed, sometimes to lower its voice and touch silence; always to rework itself in the light of what exceeds its grasp. This leads to unthreading the finely stitched web in which the political economy of capitalism, modernity and colonialism have been so tightly bound into each other trajectories. What follows proposes such a practise, where cutting and undoing the stitches can hopefully suggest other and more sustainable configurations of time, place and belonging. This is not about an alternative knowledge, but rather an alternative configuration of what constitutes knowledge—itself an ongoing process—as a profoundly political and historical question.

In the calligraphy of thought and associated critical practices, writing is never merely the means of a rational and transparent communication. The very gesture of registering time and space instals a limit and reasons a border that is integral to the act of articulation.[31] It constitutes a discontinuity, an interval or cut, where a critical trace dispossesses the gesture of arrival of any conclusive understanding. This, to borrow from the South African artist William Kentridge, leaves us with an uncertain grammar of the world that proposes the recognition of 'a space of not knowing'.[32] In the inherited materiality of the planet, beyond the limited rationalism of self-confirming thought, there always remains an opening on a future yet to come. It is perhaps here that Occidental thought and its philosophy begins to slip beyond a Platonic framing of the world, and an associated obsesssion with the question of Being, to acknowledge that the real question lies in the precise, hence political, *historicity* of its languages, practices and institutions.

NOTES

1. Berger and Mohr 2010, 104. The book was originally published in 1975.
2. Scott, 2004, 15.
3. Wolfe 2006, 394.
4. Ascione, 2016.
5. Kureishi, 2005,92.
6. Hickle, 2015.
7. Todorov, 1992. For further details, see Madley, 2015.
8. Quijano, 2000.
9. Elhaik, 2016.
10. Hallaq, 2014. See also Hallaq, 2013.
11. Birnbaum, 2016,16.
12. Adorno and Horkheimer, 2016. The quotes are drawn from the Preface to the 1969 edition.
13. Giroux, 2004.
14. Castoriadis, 2009.
15. Peters and Bulut, 2011.
16. Harney and Moten 2013.
17. Césaire 1972.
18. This emerges in a telling manner in a discussion of the hypothesis of a 'non-colonial knowledge' with the noted American academic Ann Laura Stoler, conducted in 2015 by Martina Tazzioli and Oliver Belcher: Stoler, Tazzioli, Belcher 2015. In the end, Stoler shields the academic apparatus from the consequences of this possibility.
19. Oberoi 2015.
20. Mellino 2013.
21. Wolfe, 2004.
22. Bourriaud, 1998.
23. Berger, 1972; Didi-Huberman, 2000.
24. Fanon 1986.
25. Smith, 2012.
26. In Birnbaum, 2016, 20.
27. Birnbaum, 2016,16.
28. Birnbaum, 2016, 20, 22.
29. Butler, 2012,128.
30. D'Eramo, 2013, 26.
31. Mutman, 2014.
32. Rosenthal 2009, 67.

Chapter Two

A Broken Archive

When Renaissance man became the measure of the universe and inaugurated the modern world view he also inaugurated the mechanisms that translated the planet into a world picture. The gender is deliberate. And if, as Heidegger affirmed, it is here, and for the first time, that the world is fully framed and becomes a picture, the patriarchal logic that supervised teleological faith, even if transferred from divine providence to private belief and secular progress (or, even better, mixed together) continues to set the pulse. This modality of representation, initially developed in the pictorial perspective of the Renaissance and then most fully promoted in the sixteenth-century proliferation of cartography and maps, mirrored back to Europe *its* measure of the world. At this point, and beyond Heidegger and the spaces that solely reflect European thought, there lies the world that resists and remains intractable to the logic of such maps and understandings. Invariably considered non-modern and underdeveloped, and correspondingly located in extra-European time and territory, the revaluation of the present that arrives from there radically undoes the securities and separation of the here. This revaluation, in play since first contact five centuries ago, is the critical heart of a decolonised postcolonial criticism. To borrow from the critical lexicon of Walter Benjamin, here the postcolonial operates a cut in time, a slash across those empty chronologies that are unable to house fractures, dissonance, asymmetrical relationships of power, intervals and the shifting assemblages of unfolding conjunctures.

This is clearly a very different understanding of the 'postcolonial' from that proposed in a simple chronology where postcoloniality seemingly succeeds and absolves the colonial (despite all the evidence to the contrary). The argument pursued here is that the postcolonial is most pertinent precisely in understanding the West and its continuing appropriation of the world. What are under consideration are the very mechanisms of culture and power that gave rise to the colonial and imperial world, and its centrality to the formation of Occidental modernity. This is not simply about colonial history, area studies and the regionalisation of the globe into zones of expertise (and ultimately intellectual and political management). Rather, it is about engaging critically with the practices and politics of a particular will to power that transformed the world into a colonial enterprise, providing persistent geographies that continue to map and produce the performative political cues for the present. It arrives at an understanding of modernity whose historical and cultural formation is intrinsically colonial in its premises and predatory practices.[1]

The undertow at work here transposes that specific history into a diverse critical frame that refuses a unique Occidental accounting of time and space. So, the postcolonial here is understood to involve an *ongoing* confrontation with a colonial legacy and its impact on the present. This is precisely what is obscured by a historicism that thinks the world has now emancipated itself from political, cultural and economic colonisation by the West. The postcolonial is not just after colonialism, but rather involves the radical revaluation of the political economy of a capitalist making whose formation and continuation is dependent on colonialism as a historical process and as a *continuing* cultural and political order. This is to insist on the persistence of colonialism in our midst. It is these violent mechanisms that the West unleashed on the world that have maintained the West as the West, as distinct from the rest of the planet. Stuart Hall most effectively caught this meshing of time and place undoing the (colonial) distinctions the Occident has always sought to maintain:

> It follows that the term 'post-colonial' is not merely descriptive of 'this' society rather than 'that', or of 'then' and 'now'. It re-reads 'colonisation' as part of an essentially transnational and transcultural 'global' process—and it produces a decentered, diasporic or 'global' rewriting of earlier, nation-centred imperial grand narratives. Its theoretical values therefore lies precisely in its refusal of this 'here' and 'there', 'then' and 'now', 'home' and 'abroad' perspective.[2]

To pursue this line of thought is also to announce a scepticism towards the idea that the revolutionary uprisings that swept across substantial parts of the Arab world in 2011 announced the conclusion of the postcolonial as a critical apparatus for understanding the politics and culture of present-day planetary modernity.[3] Reducing the postcolonial to the single temporality that marked the post-independent and often authoritarian regimes that replaced colonial administration misses its multi-layered complexities and its precise critique of existing chronologies. The postcolonial is what precisely allows us to conjoin diverse temporalities and locations in a coeval critical configuration. This cuts into the world—both past and present—that produced, managed and lived the colonial in multiple ways. It provides, in my opinion, crucial critical leverage for opening up the colonial archives of modernity. Clearly interest lies not in seeking abstractedly to hold on to, or defend, the term 'postcolonial', but rather in insisting on the historical processes, cultural relations and political configurations that postcolonial criticism helps us to identify.

WHOSE SPACE, WHOSE TIME?

The thought that claims universality consistently betrays logics, laws and languages that are intimately located in a historical and cultural configuration that we can call Occidental modernity. Here we confront a *precise* political economy that since the inception of European ascendancy on a global scale has persistently sought to world the world in its image. The outcome is that such concepts as *human, wealth, nature, markets, progress, history* and *development*, while being presented as though timeless and given, are rather the historically situated products of a continual working up of the world into a particular conceptual register that reflects a culturally elaborated set of social relations and powers. The naturalisation of such terms and their subsequent global application underwrites a colonial enterprise and the effective management of asymmetrical relationships of power, while all the time reconfirming the historical rationality for such asymmetry, and hence the intrinsic necessity to continue to reproduce that modality of historical reason. This double bind in which 'history' continues to produce the explanations of history without being subjected to a critical interruption or 'decolonisation' of its own historicity ensures that it remains the unique and universal repository of truth, knowledge and power.

It is along the edges of such an argument that we can begin to contest the global management of the space and time of the contemporary world, together with its particular construction of the past. Here we can identify the necessary contestation of European templates that have ensured a subsequent stranglehold on critical definitions and associated political practices. The assured manner with which Europe applies the conceptual frames of freedom, humanism, democracy and revolution in explaining the world has clearly been contested in the actions and ideas of precisely those who have struggled against its verdicts. Here is James Baldwin bluntly capturing this historical myopia:

> All of the Western nations are caught in a lie, the lie of their pretended humanism; this means that their history has no moral justification, and the West has no moral authority.[4]

Anti-colonialism and national liberation struggles have historically not only turned that language inside out to reveal its hypocritical intent, but also more recent events such as the uprisings and revolts across North Africa and the Middle East have profoundly reiterated the political (and epistemological) stakes involved. I will return to this point in the following chapters.

The idea of clear differences endorsed by geography and time—'orientalism' to coin a term—now fall away when, for example, we acknowledge the three monotheisms of Christianity, Judaism and Islam as being deeply sedimented in the complex making of modern Europe. Historically and culturally they are internal, and not external to its constitution. At the end of the day, discussing democracy, freedom, faith and progress we find ourselves confronting, often repressed, historical and cultural processes, not categorical truths. This does not mean simply sustaining the anthropological banality that they do things differently elsewhere. Rather, it is to insist that our conceptual language is susceptible to being traversed by a radical inquiry that queries the historicism that continues to endorse only *our* position in the world.

Such constructions, most explicit in the power of European political geography to divide and define the world, obviously produces the distance from subaltern souths according to the historical powers that assume the global north to be the unique legislator of a planetary modernity. The assumption is that modernity has its roots and origins in the West. Attention to historical detail might actually tell us another story. Since the fall of Rome Europe was a periphery trying to catch up with the rest of Eurasia. Its subsequent modernity was largely assembled from technological and cultural developments already achieved elsewhere. This was often achieved through the deliberate devastation of economic competition and political resistance: the destruction of indigenous economies and the importation of slaves in the Americas, the dismantling of the Indian textile industry in favour of northern English mills, the military imposition of opium imports against the will of the Chinese government, just to cull some key examples. If since the fifteenth century the fact that Europe has violently imposed its will on the rest of the planet is uncontroversial, what it actually collated into 'modernity' was not the only possibility in circulation. It was precisely the perpetual violence of military conquest, genocide, slavery and the juridical insistence of individual property as the sources of recognised rights—all bound up in the programmed destruction of other modes of production in order to create what Nicos Poulantzas called a 'global mode of production' for markets abroad and industries at home—that has sanctioned this particular modality of modernity right down to the present.[5]

In this critical interruption we can tap into deeper histories that draw out and replay the consensual accounting of time. Here we discover that the Islamic and Arab world is not outside the formation of European modernity but rather inscribed directly in its making. The histories of Spain, Sicily and the Balkans are inconceivable without the recognition of this inheritance. As the recent research of Hans Belting has recently proposed, even the mathematical and scientific bases of perspective, the epistemological fulcrum of Italian and European humanism, were anticipated by Arab philosophy and science. The research in eleventh-century Cairo by Ibn al-Haythan, known in Europe as Alhazen, elaborated the premises that were subsequently applied to the visual arts in Florence some four centuries later.[6] Such jumps in time, slides and variations within a genealogical account of different cultural traditions, produce multiple temporalities in the field of understanding, rendering its formation altogether more extensive and less parochial.

Despite its obvious cultural and historical specificity, modern Western thought has historically had the power to impose itself as universal. All other systems of thought and intelligence are invariably localised as traditions: sources of potential anthropological, not epistemological, interest. This is clearly the result not of thought per se but of powers presented in the abstract reach of reason. It reveals the fundamentalism of Occidentalism as it proposes the unique path to the truth. To adopt a critical position within this inheritance means to cut across earlier boundaries and propose very different maps. In place of the well-worn parabola of Europe commencing in ancient Athens and arriving in nineteenth-century London before bouncing across the Atlantic, we could choose to follow the advice of the great fourteenth-century historian Ibn Khaldun and break open such symmetries of time and place. If Ibn Khaldun's *The Muqaddimah. An Introduction to History* (1377) clearly preceded the modern, nationalist framing of historiography, its method also exceeds it. It encourages us, for example, to consider the Mediterranean of his time not only in terms of Italian maritime state mercantile power or the Spanish *Reconquista*, but also along other axes that stretch eastwards into Persia and south into West Africa. This is the sort of perspective that will be echoed six centuries later in Shalom Dov Goitein's five-volumed *A Mediterranean Society*.[7] In a similar vein, George Makdisi's work on the rise of humanism in classical Islam and the Christian West underscores a complex web of interactions that refuses to be drawn into a singular cultural or religious domain.[8] More recently there is Lisa Lowe encouraging us to think in terms of the modern historical intimacy of the four continents of Europe, Africa, Asia and the Americas in establishing the planetary premises for European liberalism and empire.[9]

All of this is to suggest an idea of modernity that does not simply emanate outwards from its presumed source in the West. Rather, as Walter Mignolo and others have argued, we are encouraged to think of a spatial-temporal series of combinations, forged in an agonistic planetary frame, in which the production of modern 'Europe' is structurally dependent upon what it historically negates and culturally represses. If, as Enrique Dussel and Dipesh

Chakrabarty suggest, this regionalises and provincialises Europe, it also, as Ranjit Guha has forcibly argued, unwinds the Hegelian historicisation of the world. The prospect that renders History and Europe one, and its unilateral consequences on the subsequent definitions and deployment of the concepts of citizenship, freedom, revolution, democracy and subjectivity, begins to enter a more complex dimension. A claimed universalism is now confronted with the inaugural violence that established the planet as the picture of European subjectivity and the ensuing objectification of the world in its mirror image. It was colonialism and the brutal subjugation of the globe that most tellingly sustained Europe as the presumed source of modernity. If this is the inevitable barbarism that accompanies every 'document of civilisation' (Walter Benjamin), once explicitly written into the score it leads to a very different understanding of the historical tuning of the modern world.

Wresting modernity away from the West, not so much to engage in the impossible cancellation of that hegemonic narrative as to displace its presumptuous centrality, is to rewrite the composition. Rewrite, not cancel: Occidental thought cannot simply be discarded; it commands our lexicons and the legitimation of sense, it is hegemonic. However, it can and must be reworked. Thus, this is not the reforming prospect of the perspective of a multiple modernity that still leaves Europe and the West at the core. Rather, it presents us with an altogether more tattered, contaminated and volatile constellation where we are routed through diverse roots that render global processes both concrete and specific. Here historical and cultural differences, transmitted and transmuted via continual translation, lead to a mobile, fractal geography. As Santiago Castro-Gómez insists, this means to dethrone the abstract Euro-American legitimacy of globalisation and its exercise of the existing hierarchies of power.[10] This altogether more complex inheritance, with its double consciousness of both Europe and the rest of the world, proposes the global not in terms of a stable map with its chartable circuits and flows, but as an altogether rougher, uneven, frequently opaque, series of overlapping territories and interactive borderscapes, that promote 'border thinking' (Mignolo) and adopting the 'border as method' (Mezzadra and Neilson).[11]

EUROPE'S DARK MIRROR

The struggle for a historical future necessarily involves a struggle for the past that interrogates the interpretation and explanation of the present. Against a European metaphysics that negates its historical location and formation in the name of an abstract and universal reason, today's excluded world cannot simply represent a reaction or refusal of a hegemonic knowledge formation. Rather, it promotes a geopolitics of knowledge that challenges the seeming objectivity of the social sciences, and queries a philosophy of uninterrupted Occidental lineage. Let us recall Frantz Fanon's point here: 'For the colonised subject, objectivity is always directed against him'.[12] The presumed neutrality of the language employed veils an epistemology of violence that colonises ontology in an implicit racial order.[13] It produces the colonised silence that surrounds the drive to conclusively analyse and explain the modern world.

In this inherited scenario there exists the persistence of place and the insistence of the location of culture. Since 1500, space and power, no matter how immediate the coordinates, have been articulated by Europeans in global modalities.[14] With the perspective from afar ensuring a universal picture, the complexities of the foreign world of natives and nature could be reduced to the dumb and objective site of resources and reason. The nucleus of the question lies here: to arrive at understanding the world commencing from the a priori of abstract reason, or to arrive at knowledge commencing from the world in which thinking is a social process, a historical relation? This is perhaps to phrase the question too starkly, too harshly. Still as we bump against the body of the European Enlightenment it helps us to clarify a potential cleavage in politically and historically thinking the world. Contesting the epistemology of Occidental modernity that understands reality through the will of its being is to comprehend that in capturing the world in the net of its reason it is all too easy to forget that the net is also full of holes.[15] In fact, the net is predominantly constituted by those empty spaces, those gaps. Objectification and the desire to render the world transparent to reason inevitably falls through them. Perhaps such limits—historically formed and culturally inscribed—need to be explicitly brought into the frame.[16] Recently, Gennaro Ascione has effectively captured this situation in a compact image:

> In the epistemic territory of social thought, the reiteration of the western canon with its fundamental categories is instrumental in confining colonial subjecthood together with its counter-hegemonic standpoints within the boundaries of an epistemological apartheid.
> To preserve the colonizer's privileges in the realm of the production of knowledge, conceptual boundaries are tightly patrolled: what refuses to conform to dominant social thought, exceeding its horizons and questioning its authority, is rejected beyond the borders of concept formation; its theoretical constituency flattened with the compliant tone of paternalism or tinged with the caricatural palette of exoticism.[17]

After 1492, the alterity of the Americas and the ethnic cleansing of Spain established Europe as the pinnacle of a homogeneously conceived historical 'progress', endorsed in the subsequent racial hierarchisation of the rest of the planet. The brutal simplicity proposed here carries much contemporary political and popular weight. The modern Western concept of race is profoundly entwined in the European discovery of the Americas and is central to its colonial appropriation of the world.[18] The assumed inferiority of native America, Asia, Africa and Australasia is the cultural and scientific object through which European subjectivity reproduced and renovated itself. The racism that underwrites the subsequent hierarchisation of knowledge, leaving the West as the unique legislator, was initially experimented and developed in the discovery and colonisation of the New World (although already incubated in the wars of Christendom against the Muslim world). Behind the profound hypocrisy of European humanism, and the abstract mechanisms of recognition and disavowal inscribed within the Occidental genealogy of the human and social sciences, lie the *indios* and the black slave. Today, that history, modernity's heart of darkness, returns to haunt the world picture, rattle the frame, tear the map, cross and confute the explanations we are accustomed to apply. What precisely has been excluded in order for a particular regime of knowledge (and power) to pass now constitute the contemporary spectres of modernity. Drawing upon unauthorised registers, and their particular understandings of a world forged in the light of colonial violence, these now disseminate other knowledges. They promote what Ian Baucom has called the ethical instance of refusing to let the past die.[19] The latter continues to pile up in the present.[20] Inscribed in death and disappearance, that which Achille Mbembe nominates as the necropolitics of modernity—deployed on the racialised objects of yesterday's slavery and in today's immigration laws—challenges, as James Baldwin once put it, the moral claims of the West on the world.[21]

Here the authority of a stable historicism, apparently able to establish the facts and identify the documents, is destined to be drawn into wider circuits where the 'method' that permits its exercise of knowledge (and power) can no longer pass unchallenged. There is, as Victoria Browne argues, an altogether denser and more multi-layered ground that is being crossed here, and it remains irreducible to a single accounting of time and an associated objectivity. Conflicting narratives of the past mine not only hidden histories. They also introduce unruly accountings of temporalities that queer the authoritative and patriarchal framing of the calendar and challenge its systematic framing of the present (and the future).[22]

The putative universality of the postcolonial revaluation and reconfiguration of modernity lies in the condensed critical instance of its planetary interconnectedness and common (however detailed in difference, location and rhythm) formation. This, I would argue, is a historical condition. Its universality is an ambivalent, heterogeneous condition and constellation, rather than a neat conceptual order or definition. This also means, and developing the argument proposed by David Scott, that I remain interested in the 'point' of postcolonial criticism rather than in a scholarly evaluation of its 'meaning'.[23] If the paradigm of postcolonial studies has seemingly lost the edge of a paradigm shift in the Anglo-American academy, this is certainly by no means the case in continental Europe, where its critical cut and disruption of the agenda of the social and human sciences has still largely to be registered.[24] Of course, the whole argument of paradigm shifts and their orders of truth, borrowed from T.S. Kuhn and Michel Foucault, could also be extended to the academic apparatus and its consensual reproduction of scholarly values and criteria. Here, as I suggested in the preceding chapter, postcolonial criticism, even when blunted by institutional accommodation, potentially touches a far deeper nerve in insisting on the provincialisation of a historical knowledge formation that passes for global and universal.

Against ideas of disciplinary 'neutrality' and 'balanced' evaluations, inherited from nineteenth-century European certitude and an accompanying liberal order, the critical point of the postcolonial is to disseminate a series of black holes in the universe of the social and human sciences. By that I mean a series of interrogations and problematics that the existing disciplinary arrangement of knowledge has not authorised and structurally seeks to negate. This dark matter is the underside of the transparency that the social sciences pursue, believing that the truth can be fully represented, measured and caught by its disciplinary will.[25] Such methodological premises unconsciously intersect with an increasingly neoliberal cartography that operates in the belief that the world is as flat as a map. The dematerialised universals of intellectual provenance are invariably the flipside of a political economy secured in the abstract commodification of life (both human and non), where difference and specificity find a generalised equivalence in the unshackled circulation of capital.

Contesting the automatic correlation of knowledge with the West, seemingly endorsed in a unilateral flow from Europe towards the rest of the planet, draws us, as Naomi Sakai has pointed out, into considering an 'archaeology of colonial modernity'.[26] For if the West, as concept and historical configuration, can only sustain itself through identifying and subordinating the non-West via violent contact and colonisation, then whatever critical thought comes out of Asia, Africa or Latin America is destined to encounter resistance and refusal. As Sakai puts it, 'it is impossible to overlook the fact that the classification of knowledge is intimately correlated with the classification of mankind'.[27] Subordinated to the universality of Western science other voices can only be recognised within these protocols. Through a rigid codification of time and space, other knowledges can only pass wearing the mask of the Occidental academy, respecting its rules, promoting its premises. If not they are consigned to being non-modern, local and particular: 'back there' and 'out there'. To admit to their coeval presence would be to destabilise a certain idea of modernity and displace the authority that establishes the tempo-spatial distance that guarantees the centrality of Occidental epistemology. For if this state of affairs no longer holds, then the presumed linearity of progress towards a unique modernity pioneered by the West becomes untenable in both historical and critical terms.

The translation of geography into chronology, of the non-Occidental world into the backward, underdeveloped, not-yet modern, is a temporal and spatial operation that depends upon controlling the definitions, that is, the knowledge, of the world. Further, as Bonaventura de Sousa Santos insists, it requires, despite the shallow ideology of globalisation, maintaining the division between the West and the rest of the planet. This installs what he terms 'abyssal thinking'.[28] Externalised and rendered subordinate to the Western metropole, the rest of the world cannot pretend universal recognition, only the status of the particular. The latter constitutes local belief systems. As we have seen, they can be the object of eventual anthropological and scientific enquiry, but never attain the status of abstract and universal knowledge. Their knowledge claims are rendered incomprehensible in the light of the criteria enforced on them via a violent act of translation that leaves them speechless. At this point, political resistance becomes inseparable from epistemological resistance.[29]

This state of affairs endorses the right of the West to colonise and redeem the subordinated in seemingly the most neutral and rational fashion. This is directly inscribed in the universal pretensions of its institutions and their monopoly on the terms of knowledge, justice, democracy and liberty. Contemporary international law is the application of the Occidental legal system on a global scale. The asymmetrical relations of power inscribed in seemingly neutral abstractions and application constitutes the arbitrary distinctions that establish the 'legal' and the 'illegal': terms that are overwhelmingly secured in the West via such crucial concepts as the 'individual' and private property. To drive this historical and critical point home, we need only ask legal for whom, where, when and how? This situation is further entrenched by the international hegemony of the linguistic limits of English to accommodate, if not actively censor, other cultural semantics.[30]

THE SOUTHS OF THE WORLD

Meanwhile, the narrow line between formal democracy and authoritarian rule everyday grows thinner as civil rights and liberties are rolled back in the name of security. The sovereignty of the rule of law slides into accommodation with governability. Between fears of terrorism and continuing financial vandalism, it seems we are in a state of meltdown. The idealism that launched and recruited many to the project of the European Union has been transformed into the implacable law of the market whose rationality is apparently irrefutable. It becomes increasingly clear that only by bringing into play what the official institutions of Europe have structurally sought to exclude, can the continent, its histories, cultures and politics, be productively taken apart and transformed into a further set of political possibilities. This means acknowledging that the European Union has been captured by global capitalism and its neoliberal directives: from the juridical and cultural construction of 'immigration' to privileging the market and private enterprise over and against the vestiges of the welfare state and a defence of the commons. We are now forced to acknowledge that even for European liberalism the historical norm was not the welfare state or labour security, these represented an exception, limited to a short time span and a restricted part of the world. On the contrary, both historically and globally, the norm is precariousness. Appeals to a Kantian cosmopolitanism to shore-up the possibilities of Europe and its enlightened tradition is now at a dead end. That inheritance is not so much over because it has been overtaken by other more powerful and cohesive players, for instance China, but rather, and more significantly due to its own internal contradictions and its failure to understand its own history.

As a universalising force, Europe drew its historical and cultural energies directly from colonialism and the racial hierarchies it employed in aggrandising and incorporating the rest of the planet. The idea that Europe has learnt from that history and can now play a decisively different role in an emergent global assemblage is wishful thinking. It is wishful thinking precisely because Europe persistently fails to consider its colonial past and thereby continues to operate in the present with precisely the same semantics as other global hegemonic forces. To undo this state of affairs would be to confront what Foucault in *The Archaeology of Knowledge* referred to as the inability of a hegemonic order to come to terms with a 'general theory of discontinuity, of series, of limits, unities, specific orders and differentiated autonomies and dependences'.[31]

The refusal to rework Europe's colonial archive is intricately bound into the insistence on the nation state as the unique placeholder of history, culture and identity. For if all of Europe was involved in the colonial project, as Joseph Conrad famously reminds us via the figure of Mr. Kurtz, then its postcolonial undoing and reconfiguration requires the unwinding of that colonial moment and the modern nation state that it permitted. Right now, Europe has become a wall against which counter-histories cast their bodies with little hope of recognition. Only by refuting and dismantling that wall can a radically diverse sense of European belonging emerge.

To undo the unilateral imposition of this dividing line is to be drawn into a revaluation of the making of the modern world. This is to understand that in order for the colonial apparatus to operate unhindered freedoms and democratic procedures elsewhere were necessarily negated. This is as valid today (and perhaps helps us better understand the structural context of the breakdown and hi-jacking of the so-called Arab Spring and the subsequent reconfirmation of authoritarian neoliberalism in Egypt) as it was for the denial of the Haitian revolution by Europe and the United States at the beginning of the nineteenth century, or the European management and division of Africa in the subsequent decades (from the French invasion of Algeria in 1830 to the European carve up of the continent at Berlin in 1884–1885). This is why it was the slave owners, not the slaves, who received compensatory payment after the abolition of slavery in the British Empire (leading to the biggest government pay out in British history until the financial bailout of 2008). A decade earlier the French government of Charles X had demanded payment of the modern equivalent of $21 billion from Haiti. The sum, subsequently reduced to two-thirds, was based on the calculation of compensation for the property, including the market value of the slaves, the European owners had 'lost'. The claim was enforced by French war ships and the threat of invasion. This imposed 'independence debt' was to cripple the Haitian economy for decades. The sum was finally liquidated in 1893, eighty-nine years after Haiti had achieved independence from France.

Here it is important to emphasise that I am not seeking to propose the counter-balance of the non-Occidental world against the north of the planet, but rather attempting to loosen, if not disband, the logics and languages that hold those relations in place. If this points us towards a possible 'epistemology of the south', it also clearly exceeds any simple geographical location.[32] The south here is a mobile placeholder. It conjoins multiple localities and temporalities, from the zones of rural poverty in nineteenth-century Europe that conjoins Scandinavia, Scotland and Ireland with Italy and Greece, to the colonial rampage unleashed by Europe on Africa, Asia and the Americas since 1500. Stretching from the characterisation of the perceived underdevelopment and barbarism of southern Europe by northern visitors in the eighteenth century, and elsewhere deployed in the colonial worlds of Africa, Asia and Latin America, its linear location in time and geography today quickly unravels. Global migration, both within and outside Euro-America, combined with the neoliberal delegitimisation of labour rights and the promotion of precarious livelihood, produces a south within every metropole. So the critical trope is planetary in scope. It pretends a universality while all the time stitched into localities sustained in profoundly unequal relations of power. This other side of our seemingly universal reason, which carries the dimly perceived threat of us being potentially reasoned in another fashion, draws us into the exposed space of the postcolonial condition.

The south is a critical intention. This affirmation is not intended simply to repropose geopolitical and economic distinctions embodied in the existing souths of the world. It is also to consider in intellectual and cultural, hence political, terms what tends to lie beyond recognition by the north of the planet. It is to consider what, although in the shadows, is simultaneously essential to the inequitable relations of power that structure the modern world. So, these distinctions do not serve to indicate merely metaphorical spaces. They speak of insurrectionary languages and practices, emerging from the multiple souths of the planet: from decolonialising struggles in Asia and Africa to the voices of Frantz Fanon, James Baldwin and the Black Panthers, from Palestine to Northern Ireland, from indigenous struggles in Latin America and India to ecological awareness and protest. This broad and interwoven front of struggles, and the global perspectives they support, if immediately political in scope are also of fundamental epistemological importance. They query the edifice of Occidental reason and its institutions. They expose its foundations to unsuspected questions. They render its universal pretensions altogether more precise and locatable in time and space.

Thus, to think with the south is not only to point to the historical and cultural evidence of how the West underdeveloped the rest of the planet over many centuries of Occidental rule. It is also to register how the present-day constitution of European institutions and identities, its democracy, knowledge and subject formation, is sustained and reproduced through that history. The modern metropolis is replete with colonial reminders in its monuments to earlier colonial wars, and in its present-day multicultural inhabitants, music, religions and cuisine. However, this obvious sociology betrays an altogether profounder historical hubris. The colonial fashioning of the modern world has not simply passed away. The very making of the modern political economy, the accumulation of wealth and the colonial divisions of the planet in the endless pursuit of capital in a world made market by the West, continues. There have been other empires, other violent exploitations and divisions, but never before on a scale induced by a mode of production that requires the planet as the measure of its wealth, accumulation and power.

Such an intricate entanglement of the shared universalism of European humanism, colonialism and capitalism finds its political realisation in Occidental liberalism. Property, and its instrumental improvement (hence indigenous understandings of the land and territory are excluded from consideration precisely for being unproductive), was inscribed in ideas of political rights and liberties secured in law.[33] Ultimately politics, in promoting individual wealth and happiness as presumably coterminous conditions, becomes the missionary advocate for the systematic imperatives of the economy where the common good is promoted through individual enterprise. This forms the modern canon of Western political thought, both its historical practices, juridical framework and overarching metaphysics. Reduced to its bare bones, the public power of the state is expected to protect and promote the private power of property. Political theory itself represents the successful subtraction and subordination of the discourse of rights and regulations to the transcendent rule of the economy. The only end of the economy is the economy, not the attainment of social and political improvement. Set out in distinct spheres, disciplines and sciences, politics is cleaved from the economic. As

Carl Schmitt with characteristically brutal clarity pointed out, this is to pose the economic as an essentially apolitical matter and politics as being involved in essentially non-economic concerns. In this manner, he continues, economic expansion and the exploitation of natural resources can be considered pacific, non-political processes.[34] Exploitation—of nature, of other human beings—is productive. It is therefore morally right and natural. Government is bound to safeguard and promote such actions. Presented as progress, politics provides the legalised violence for endorsing and guaranteeing the freedom of economic power.

Such understandings of the political order have historically been secured through the brutal negation of other, frequently non-property-owning individuals, groups and classes and the denial of their understandings of freedom and justice: from the expropriation of indigenous lands and slave labour to chattel servitude and women's domestic labour.[35] Our particular framing of the world though the application of such understandings of liberal freedom has clearly been attained through the negation of freedom to others. This was already apparent in the 1640s in the English Revolution. The Diggers, Levellers and the Putney Debates in the New Model Army in the autumn of 1647 witnessed opposition to the privilege of property and an insistence on the sovereignty of the poor and rights to the commons. It was ultimately defeated. The riotous army was despatched to colonial conquest and massacres in Ireland. The language that was forged on that occasion nevertheless flowed into the currents of the revolutionary Atlantic and the hidden histories of modernity to forge a resistant lexicon of rights and freedoms.[36]

Here, in another maritime world, is how Amitav Ghosh describes the arrival of the Portuguese in the Indian Ocean at the end of the fourteenth century:

> Having long been accustomed to the tradesman's rules of bargaining and compromise they tried time and time again to reach an understanding with the Europeans—only to discover, as one historian has put it, that the choice was 'between resistance and submission; cooperation was not offered'. Unable to compete in the Indian Ocean by purely commercial means, the Europeans were bent on taking control of it by aggression, pure and distilled, by unleashing violence on a scale unprecedented on those shores. As far as the Portuguese were concerned, they had declared a proprietorial right over the Indian Ocean: since none of the peoples who lived around it had thought to claim ownership of it before their arrival, they could not expect the right of free passage in it now.[37]

Time unravels from a single spool. The past becomes proximate. The world, the knowledges and practices that colonised the planet are now reassessed by histories, cultures and lives that were previously unauthorised to comment. Our account comes undone as the past refuses to pass or respect our verdict on its present meaning. Seeking to listen and learn from this situation is perhaps to recognise that it is precisely in the heartlands of the Occident that postcolonial criticism most sharply acquires its historical cultural and political pertinence. It is here that the historical hybridisation of the planet which ensures that no culture or identity is 'pure' or uncontaminated, finally comes home to roost.

This is not me speaking from or for the south, but rather insisting on listening and learning from what arrives from the seemingly elsewhere to disrupt the securities of my language and the stabilities of my vision. For if history does not simply pass but rather accumulates in an unresolved present then historical time can no longer be considered purely linear and homogeneous. This brings us close to the Walter Benjamin's figure of a historical constellation casting shifting illuminations into the present. It also brings us into the vicinity of Reinhart Koselleck's proposal of the multiple, heterogeneous and interdependent articulations of time that do not necessarily arrive at a unique and absolute reality.[38] As Sandro Mezzadra and Federico Rahola capture it:

> Postcolonial critique intervenes on this point specifically. On the one hand, it does so with a somewhat traditional gesture directed towards the past, or rather, to a past, that of slavery and the mute, non-dialectical violence of colonial domination. Insofar as this past resists any possibility of compensation with respect to expectations, it obstinately resists being consigned to the past, and populates the present with ghosts. On the other hand, postcolonial criticism invests this same present with a critique of 'historicism', such as the one proposed by Dipesh Chakrabarty in *Provincializing Europe*, focusing specifically on the possibility of chronologically ordering the strata of which global time is composed. In other words, it is the very temporal modality capital is forced to employ today in the construction of its History, that is Benjamin's 'homogeneous and empty' temporality, which continuously brings to the surface the plural histories that it has matched, incorporated and overwhelmed in the process of its becoming world.[39]

ARCHIVES OF MODERNITY

In this perspective, the souths of world produced through geographies of power are not simply the extension of Antonio Gramsci's noted 'southern question' on an altogether more extensive map.[40] To remain with such a perspective simply finds us drawing temporary comfort from an alternative subaltern mirror image that contests a modernity irradiating outwards from a presumed centre in the West. As a subordinated counter-image such optics inadvertently reaffirm the linearity of the historical time of Occidental 'progress' and its unrelenting measurement of the rest of the globe. The singularity of that history is suspect. Its power to render heterogeneity uniform requires a unique temporality that negates what Koselleck would call simultaneous, interdependent and heterogeneous articulations.[41] The latter lead to multiple representations that are irreducible to a unique or absolute rendering of reality. The critical challenge then becomes to consider the question in its planetary location as a moving constellation of different rhythms and conditions that overlap and intersect in an alternative understanding of a multilateral modernity that is irreducible to a single source or authority. It was Gramsci who taught us that the assumptions of an inferior south were structurally essential to the reproduction of the superior north. The south was not a discarded left over, or merely the detritus of progress, it was an essential component in the composition and reproduction of a national (and trans-national) political economy. It is here that the seemingly temporal drag, induced by the weight of social and cultural complexities and distinctions associated with multiple souths, breaks up any teleological understanding of historical time. It leads to the critical undoing of the very idea of a single modernity as it now slides into more complex and inconclusive configurations.

At the same time, adopting the global historical frame we, too, also run the danger of rendering the world flat as a map. Here not only local details are lost to view but, above all, the structural impact of asymmetrical relations of power come to be muted in a checkerboard reality in which violence, power and injustice are only rendered in the most abstract of coordinates. To sense the texture and register the grain is to appreciate the radical challenge of the global archive being always incomplete, yet to be fully recognised, registered and recorded. This means to deliberately confuse and confute the drive to render the world transparent to its will and register the waning hegemony of Occidental explanations when the world, rather than simply the West, becomes method.[42] Here, against the ruins of purportedly neutral and scientific definitions that accompanies the necessary delocalisation and denationalisation of the social sciences and the humanities, we can argue that there lies an unexpected rendezvous between the workings of many contemporary art practices that act 'as a proxy for their desired representations in politics' and an emergent historiographical problematic.[43] This comes together in the shared investigation, construction and exposure of the archives of modernity.

The modern emergence of epistemological anxieties over the discarded and refused colonial depository are clearly not only to be associated with the national archives of colonial government and rule that Laura Ann Stoler so carefully excavates and analyses in the case of Dutch Indonesia.[44] Such anxieties are also imbricated in the altogether more extensive and largely unacknowledged registers of colonialism that have structured and sustained the overall making of Occidental modernity, from the modern museum to the class room and the propagation of common sense in the daily media. For the archive not only speaks but is also a site of silence. It records what was thought and unthought. It contains, as Stoler reminds us, both directives and doubts, axioms and absences. So, while acknowledging the important specificities of individual colonial archives as institutions, practices, personnel and juridical enterprises, housed in physical buildings at home and abroad, we need also to move to an understanding of the global scale of the archives of colonialism as the fundamental foundation of the modern Occidental edifice, its economics, politics and culture. This is to make an epistemological argument about what passes for knowledge, and to register a complex, vibrant and ambiguous assemblage and its impact on how we have been taught to see, receive and judge the contemporary world. In the history of the West, and its appropriation of the world, colonialism, as Stoler suggestively puts it, is a watermark: indelible and therefore inevitably overlooked. This means to pursue, with Matthieu Renault, the profound implications of a *decolonised epistemology*.[45] It is to push postcolonial criticism into recognising both the genealogies of anti-colonial thought and struggle (both yesterday and today) while registering the aggression and force of a world still deeply imbricated in a colonial mind set, both in its political practices and in the disciplinary premises of its knowledge as an 'Occidental order of discourse'.[46]

We return to Joseph Conrad's prospect of a world that is still 'under western eyes'. The planet, even in resistance and rebellion, is still caught in that gaze, subjected to its powers, disciplined and structured by its political and cultural pedagogy. What speaks, or is silent, and lies beyond the syntax that assumes language is fully susceptible to a single order and reason, multiplies the margins of the hegemonic discourse, seeds potential disruption in the space between its pronouncements, darkens the text with unacknowledged shadows, ultimately undoes its illusions on the world. Beneath it all lies an unremitting confrontation with violence. This is the structure of a world brutally made over in Occidental languages and its accompanying lexicons of political and cultural power. There is no way that this arrangement will be placidly undone via a series of agreements and compromises. It can only be violently broken apart in order for its *own* theories and knowledges to be forced to travel into unauthorised zones of translation. There repeated and interrupted, they can begin to inhabit what Renault in his reading of Fanon, suggestively calls a 'decolonial geography of knowledge'.[47]

The very nature of memory and its institutional representation in archives has today to be radically rethought in a manner that breaks the boundaries of inherited institutional belonging. Mixing what was once separated—for example, European and Arab culture (or Christianity and Islam) in the historical fluidities of the Mediterranean, or insisting that sounds sustain histories in heard but unrecognised memories, or touching upon the accumulation of life and death on the island of Lampedusa or in Palestine—constitute archives that dramatically expose the colonial pretensions of modernity where so many human beings are consistently rendered 'external to the category of the human'.[48] While institutional archives, like contemporary Israel, are laboratories of the colonising mechanisms of modernity, walling in and fencing off the world, cataloguing and defining its contents, rendering it memories subservient to its logic and language, they cannot escape interpretation, contestation, reassembling. Sherene Seikaly forcefully captures this procedure:

> At the thin intersections of popular memory and archival practices lie the stories that people tell to make sense of the everyday. They weave these stories to shape the present, build connections to the past, and stake claims for the future. They draw on continuities. They distinguish ruptures. They attend to that pit of possibility and danger that is historical contingency. They sift through repetition to identify the singular, the new. And they build and nourish an archive: one that keeps a record of colonization and guards the will to decolonize. Gaza today, in its continuities and its ruptures, is an instance of the archive that is the Palestinian condition.[49]

All of this shifts our very understanding of the archive from the stilled order of documents, consensual understanding and seemingly established facts to registering the archive as an ongoing cultural and political practice. Here we find ourselves on the altogether more troubled ground of interpretation and the ensuing agonism that seeks truth not in the atavistic authority of the past but in the human rights of a historical and social justice still to come. Although Europe and the West presume to hold universal authority on such questions it is largely due to the insistence of the decolonising south of the world that the contemporary political lexicon has been forced to accommodate them.[50] The West itself has persistently used that rhetoric politically to twist and thwart those sought-for rights in order for them to become 'functional to the reproduction of dominant violence, and ultimately to the protection and legitimation of domination itself'.[51] If this struggle over the sense of the archive evokes Arjun Appadurai's noted observations on the archive as aspiration it also returns us to Michel de Certeau's insistence that the 'transformation of archival activity is the point of departure and the condition for a new history'.[52]

NOTES

1. Gregory 2004.
2. Hall 1996.
3. For example, Dabashi 2012. The whole debate was decisively anticipated by Stuart Hall and his responses to the earlier criticisms of the critical valency of the idea of the postcolonial launched by Arif Dirlik, Ella Shohat and Anne McClintock amongst others, in Hall 1996.
4. Baldwin 1972.
5. Poulantzas 1973, 15.
6. Belting 2010.
7. For a suggestive displacement inspired by Ibn Khaldun's work, see Mamdani 2013.

8. Makdisi 1990.
9. Lowe 2015.
10. Castro-Gómez 2002.
11. Mignolo 2011; Mezzadra and Neilson 2013.
12. Fanon 2004, 37.
13. Spivak 1988.
14. Schmitt 2006.
15. Vattimo 1988.
16. Morana and Dessel 2008.
17. Ascione 2017.
18. Mellino 2013.
19. Baucom 2005.
20. Benjamin 1969.
21. Mbembe 2001; Baldwin 1972.
22. Brown 2014.
23. Scott 2005.
24. For a trenchant criticism of the limits of postcolonial criticism created by its rapid acceptability in North American academia, see Shohat 1992.
25. See Guhin and Wyrtzen 2013.
26. Sakai 2011.
27. Sakai 2011.
28. Santos 2007.
29. Santos 2007.
30. Such hegemonies—historical, cultural and linguistic—are tellingly exposed by Lydia Liu in her interrogation of the drafting of the Universal Declaration of Human Rights of the United Nations (1947–1948) posed by the challenge to 'parochial universalism' by cultural differences and semantic untranslatability. See Liu 2014.
31. Foucault 1972, 12.
32. Santos 2014. This line of argument, generated in the critical conditions of thinking with and from the south of the world, is also explored in Connell 2007, as well as in Comaroff and Comaroff 2012. It is most consistently developed in the grouping of Latin American intellectuals — Anibal Quijano, Santiago Castro-Gómez, Catherine Walsh, Walter Mignolo — associated with decolonial thinking. See the essays in Mignolo and Escobar, 2010.
33. Watson 2015.
34. Schmitt 2015, 163.
35. Federici 2004.
36. Linebaugh and Rediker 2002. The authors also make the suggestive connection with the urban revolt against propertied privilege led by the fisherman Masaniello in Naples in the same year.
37. Ghosh 1994, 287 – 288.
38. Koselleck 2004.
39. Mezzadra and Rahola 2006.
40. Gramsci 2015.
41. Koselleck 2004.
42. Mbembe 2013b.
43. Wilson 2011, 7.
44. Stoler 2009.
45. Renault 2013, 49.
46. Renault 2013, 57.
47. Renault 2013, 51.
48. Seikaly 2014.
49. Seikaly 2014.
50. Jensen 2016.
51. Perugini and Gordon 2015, 4.
52. Appadurai 2003; de Certeau 1993 75.

Chapter Three

Migrating Modernities

The previous considerations now lead us to consider a double objective when looking at the contemporary state of Europe. One is to excavate the sites of its modernity, to consider what is buried and then quickly forgotten in order to permit a triumphant version to pass. This is to engage with a past that runs deep in the contours of the present. The other is to register the movement of modernity in a manner that exceeds arrest in a single location or definition. While we are accustomed to registering the mobility of modernity in terms of capital and its culture seemingly irradiating outwards from its presumed source in the West to invest the histories, peoples and lives of the rest of the planet, we are loath to acknowledge that there might also exist a more complex narrative that exceeds our authorisation. This would be an account that, as a minimum, acknowledges the co-existence and interpenetration of the capitalist formations of colonialism and European civil society, not to speak of the hybrid gestation of the modern world. The accumulative force of the multiple locations and sources of modernity propel our considerations elsewhere. Habitual distinctions of core and periphery, north and south, the West and the rest, but also of development, progress and underdevelopment, fall away to be folded into a multi-accented series of ultimately planetary coordinates that cut up and interrupt any singular comprehension of time and space. There is no a priori able to compress and comprehend this situation; the vehemence of such epistemological pretensions becomes critically and ethically unacceptable. The very incompleteness of our knowledge, despite its universal claims, alerts us to an altogether wider landscape, one that we are unable ever to fully frame. It is precisely at this point that other knowledges, that others, circulate, cross, configure and contest our hierarchisation of the world.

What today perhaps most forcibly brings together this negated understanding of the multiplicity of the past and the present is the figure of the contemporary migrant. For if the concept of migration is most directly associated with the ongoing socio-economic phenomenon of the physical migration of people and lives from the so-called south and periphery of the world (itself the latest chapter in the centrality of migration to the making of modernity since 1500), it also confronts us with an altogether wider political and historical challenge. The very syntax of the state, the nation, of citizenship and identity, is directly challenged by the clandestine histories of the migrant and her 'illegal' presence. The mechanisms that seemingly secure us in our 'home' are here radically exposed in all their arbitrary violence. For etched on the body of the contemporary migrant is not only the power of modern European law that regulates his or her status, frequently transforming their subjectivity into objects of 'illegality', but also the inadvertent signature of a colonial past. Here the altogether more systematic and aggressive migration of Europeans towards the rest of the planet over a period of centuries, now suitably forgotten, returns to the complex coordination of the present. We are drawn into a cruel and bloody archive where colonial expansion, brutal appropriation, enslavement and migration also provided the context of modern citizenship and the nation state. The much-vaunted mobility of capital and goods in the global market foregrounds a flux and fluidity that ultimately also draws us into understanding this altogether more subterranean historical and cultural formation.

At this point, the migrant is critically displaced from the socio-economic periphery of modernity to become central to its juridical and political constitution. This is condensed in Hannah Arendt's insistence on the right to have rights.[1] As Étienne Balibar rightly notes, this situation refutes the ideological stability of the nation state.[2] Against the desired permanency sought in inherited definitions of locality, home, national identity, tradition and belonging, modernity turns out to be a mobile constellation sustained in transit, translation and transformation. It now tells us another story. Migrating bodies, matter out of place, those fleeing destitution, war, poverty and persecution, challenge the location prepared for them in an existing order. The categories, languages, institutions and technologies that invest, identify and catalogue the migrant are themselves exposed. For it is not only the migrant who has now constantly to negotiate his or her passage in the world. The concepts, practices and institutions, the bio-politics that nominate and define the migrant also define 'us'. If such juridical-political practices propose the protection of Occidental democracy, they simultaneously also register the gaps, failures and refusals of a democracy that is structurally limited to some, excluded to others. Simply put, contemporary migration—between and beyond the nation state—proposes a profound interrogation of the very nature of the existing state forms, citizenship, government and their juridical pretensions and practices. Those most requiring human rights are excluded by the very state mechanism supposed to embody them from receiving them. Here Occidental humanism and governance is tested and found significantly wanting. Between the human and the citizen there opens a gap, patrolled by the law, into which a failed justice falls. To place at the centre of modernity the modern migrant and refugee is to register a paradox which, as Giorgio Agamben put it more than two decades ago, requires a radical rearticulation of existing political categories.[3]

At the same time, migrating modernities refer us to more than a metaphor borrowed from the abject world of contemporary migration, increasingly policed and punished through the accelerating militarisation of borders and the augmented surveillance of civil society. As a material force, as the perpetual coming and going of physical and cognitive matter in migrants and megabytes, the mobility of modernity itself undoes the presumed stability of a previous knowledge economy: both its location and locution are exposed to the uninvited movements and mutations that it supposedly engendered. Precisely here we can follow Naoki Sakai in his unfolding of the classificatory knowledges, academic disciplines and theory of the West and their hierarchical and 'geopolitical configuration of the world'. As he puts it:

> By inquiring into the archaeology of colonial modernity, we now begin to comprehend why theory had to be so intimately associated with the West. There is a figure of 'man', yet this humanity was not 'man' in general. Instead it had to be modified by an adjectival, 'European' or 'Western'. An archaeological analysis of colonial modernity thus discloses the participation of a certain humanism in modernity.[4]

Put synthetically: modernity as a constellation of practices, experiences and institutions is irreducible to its theorisation and understanding in a unique observatory. To insist on a particular historical and geographical formation that we call the West in the making of modernity is simultaneously also to register the planetary coordinates of its unilateral appropriation and worlding of the rest of the planet. In this perspective it hardly needs reminding that the nineteenth-century elaboration of the modern human and social sciences, and their binding into nationalist variations, took place within the constellation of colonialism and European imperialism. This history cannot be cancelled, but in being recognised it can be reconfigured. If the world can be laid out, flat as a map, for exploration, conquest and exploitation, we also know that peoples, histories and cultures are not equally placed. There exist concentrations of power and densities of wealth that create particular vectors and short circuits of privilege. The asymmetrical relations of power that cut up and differentiate the world in a hierarchy of economic, political and cultural values refer us to a planetary, and not a local, disposition. Clearly, the world is divided and distanced according to those who exercise the power to define, channel, control and exploit its resources. This situation, however, is consistently shadowed by a series of counter-histories. The increasingly fluid processes of bordering and control, some temporary, others altogether more enduring, produce instances of refusal and revolt, sites of counter-powers and productive assemblages that contest the semantics that insist that there is no alternative.[5] Contemporary securitocracy—in which every individual is a potential criminal—is not simply a response to terrorism, the refugee, the migrant. In the end, it is capitalism and not democracy that is being defended. The contemporary return to colonial mechanisms of control is about altogether wider threats to the political economy of the existing order. Among those threats are the imbricated histories of social refusal, political contestation and critical thought where an antagonistic history of modernity can be excavated precisely in the borderlands of their supposedly unwelcome and 'illegal' status.

THE PRISON OF LIBERALISM

This brings us to the heart of the present conjuncture in which the arguments in this book seek their pertinence. This is a historical and cultural arrangement shaped and formed by liberalism, by its understanding of the world and how to proceed in its possibilities. The key justification of the modern political ideology of liberalism is property.[6] Liberalism's complex genealogy reveals an exercise in individual freedom tied to property rights (including servants and slaves) and the refusal to be 'enslaved' by state interference in the perpetuation of that freedom. The economic as a transcendental force commands the field of juridical recognition and legalised appropriation (politics). So, this is also about a freedom restricted to those who have the rights (property) to claim it, and is therefore structurally bound to the dispossession and unfreedom of others. The revolt of the thirteen colonies in North America against the British Crown was for a liberty claimed by such individuals, certainly not for the slaves, women, indentured servants, paupers, or Native Americans. We are confronted with a freedom constructed on structural inequality. The legalised violence of modernity, inaugurated by the individual (Hobbes) privatisation of nature as property (Locke) forcibly reminds us that the colonial is contemporary.

Present-day neoliberalism is therefore not an absolute novelty. Rather it proposes a radical deepening and refiguring of the existent repertoire of Occidental liberalism through an altogether tighter twist of the screw. If, as Pierre Dardot and Christian Laval insist, the passage from liberalism to neoliberalism is the movement from some idea of democracy to its dismantling in order to better meet market criteria, then the earlier liberal compact is clearly coming undone in an accelerating series of social and economic inequalities.[7] Here, as Tiziana Terranova points out, 'the neoliberal market is significantly different from the liberal market inasmuch as, unlike the latter, it is not defined as an abstract logic of exchange among equals but as an ideal logic of competition between formal inequalities'.[8] Still in both cases to operate a fracture, to insist on an autonomy that exposes and refuses the 'inhumanity and fear' seeded by that order, is to violently subtract oneself from such a colonising structure of identification.[9] This, with Fanon, means to challenge the liberal political economy and the humanism to which it hypocritically appeals.

Here time telescopes: the seventeenth-century England of the liberal philosopher John Locke (who considered slavery to be a normal juridical condition in the constitution of the Carolinas, and expropriation to be a natural principle in the extension of 'civilisation') slides into the contemporary colonial global order: temporarily distinct but conceptually cogent. In both cases, the 'absolute power' (Locke) of property guarantees liberty and legitimates political authority. Once secured in philosophical and juridical terms, this becomes the lynchpin of the political economy of capital. The extension of the inalienable right to property stretches so far as to justify the extermination of those who sought to contest its exercise. Such an order is a profoundly bio-political one. Racism and the structural subordination of the non-European is not a by-product of a now superseded historical affair in which the conquest of territories and bodies were conjoined and justified, but remains central to the maintenance of present-day powers. Racial profiling and the targeting of non-whites is persistently pursued in the contemporary policing of the modern, Occidental metropolis: from London to Los Angeles, from Ferguson, Missouri, to Florence, Italy.

The savagery of the law in the defence of property and political power—leading to an explosion in capital punishment and penal transportation to the colonies—notoriously characterised eighteenth-century Britain.[10] In the Americas, a brutal colonial appropriation that arrived at genocide, together with chattel slavery and the plantation economy, was not a bloody footnote to Western progress. As Eric Williams methodically argued in *Capitalism and Slavery* (1944), slavery was central to the capitalist mode of production in the very moment that European economic and political power was brutally perfected in these colonial spaces. Such arguments, insisting on the organisation of slave labour as the prototype of the modern proletariat, had also been laid out by C.L.R. James in *The Black Jacobins: Touissant L'Ouverture and the San Domingo Revolution* (1938). As sites of 'primitive accumulation' and the systematic organisation of property-less labour the colonies were the hub of an emerging world order. If slavery was subsequently considered to be morally reprehensible (particularly in the country that was the greatest slave owner in the world—Great Britain—but which would continue to benefit from slave labour long after its official abolition), the logic that reduced others to property, and individuals to dehumanised units of abstract labour power, continues unabated. The long, and unfinished, struggle of women, the civil rights movements, and anti-colonial revolt, rebellion and resistance to modify and disband that philosophical, political and profoundly racist arrangement, is ultimately a struggle against European liberalism and its protocols of inequality. Abstracted in juridical, philosophical and political theses, the extreme discriminatory violence of the formation of modern liberal democracy and its inevitable shaping of the present world passes largely unremarked. Or else it is siphoned off into historical accounts whose political import remain muted, safely restricted to academic quarters and seemingly water-tight historical moments. However, if classical European liberalism is considered to be the model and guarantee of human progress, then the insistence on property, power, racism and colonialism clearly suggest very different and altogether more uncomfortable coordinates. It leads to a diametrically opposed understanding of the political ideology of liberalism and the colonial genealogy of the present.

Historically speaking, the transference of landed property to financial gain and commercial profit, and the passage of the revenue of rural estates and slave plantations to industrial and financial capital and urban life styles and culture artefacts, accompanied by the passage from local peasantry to the national and international labour market, is a constant tendency in the formation of the modern political economy since 1500. In the planetary processes induced by capitalist accumulation there are obviously many regional differences, within the nation as well as beyond its frontiers. Some would call them time-lags and apply the terminology of backwardness and underdevelopment to explain their presence. Here history is apparently a train called Progress that carries us into the future. However, when slavery co-exists with the foundation of republican democracy, as in the Atlantic world of the eighteenth and nineteenth centuries, and feudal land ties with the establishment of modern industrial plant, as in Italy in the first half of the twentieth century, it is perhaps critically more instructive to consider their socio-political interaction and historical complementarity. Rather than assume that one dimension (modern, democratic and industrial) is separate and superior to the negative survival of the seemingly pre-modern and archaic histories of slavery and feudalism we need to consider their being coeval. And if we are understanding these to be planetary, and not merely national, conditions and forces, then we are required to recognise this dissonant and heterogeneous history to be integral to modernity; that is, to be *the* history of modernity itself.

This helps us fully to appreciate that the violent accumulation of capital does not simply lie back there with slave labour, colonialism and the racist imposition of European hegemony, or with expropriation of the commons, the expulsion of the peasantry and subsequent enclosure by a land-owning class seeking to invest its gains elsewhere (in the colonies, in industry, in buildings, transport and cultural goods).[11] It continues. There is no simple passage from an original or primitive accumulation to a subsequently more civil and ordered one. Scottish crofters despatched to Canada after the crushing of the Jacobite rebellion of 1745 and the clearing of the Highlands, peasants moving from the rural south of Italy to Milan and the Alfa Romeo factory in the 1950s and 1960s (the subject of Luchino Visconti's 1961 film, *Rocco and His Brothers*), present-day Chinese labour migrating in millions from rural areas to the high-tech belts of Guangdong, Shaanxi, Qingdao and Shenzhen, are part of the same temporal-spatial configuration. In other words, the creative destruction and transformation of territory and time by capital produces a mobile configuration of effects on a planetary level that cannot be simply reduced to the linear succession of circles of development irradiating out from a primary centre in Europe.

The resources that went into European development, as the history of modern racial slavery so powerfully portrays (both in the capital extracted from its labour *and* the capital realised in its abolition and compensatory payments), always depended on a planetary network of conquest, exploitation and authoritarian management.[12] Dispossession, expropriation and the rigid control of land, law and political license are not simply the prerogative of seventeenth-century England and life in the North American colonies as justified by John Locke; they are very much part of our world today. This 'original' violence persists—from seeking to patent medicinal plants to bulldozing villages and towns into dams.[13] Behind all this lies the continual exploitation of unpaid female domestic labour in the 'private' sector of family life. Silvia Federici has proposed that this 'primitive accumulation' is not merely, as Marx claimed, a preliminary necessary stage for the initial start-up of capitalism, but is rather the fundamental characteristic of capitalism itself. In order to perpetuate itself, capitalism requires a constant infusion of expropriated resources and wealth.[14] In this context, the historical struggle to sustain and defend the commons against enclosure and privatisation invites us to consider capitalism not in terms of the defeat and liberation from feudalism, but rather as a reactionary move by powerful interests to retain and extend their machinery of expropriation. This line of argument has been elaborated in much of the history from below: from E.P. Thompson's classic *The Making of the English Working Class* to the vibrant radical instances drawn together in Peter Linebaugh and Marcus Rediker's *The Many-Headed Hydra. Sailors, Slaves, Commoners, and the Hidden History of the Revolutionary Atlantic*. As Kalyan Sanyal has also argued, such a war for property and individualised ownership constitutes the very reproduction of capital itself: it is not a trace of the past, but rather the unstable universality of capital oriented towards colonising the future.[15] So, rather than linear and localised transitions to accumulation we confront disturbing transformations that reach through a mosaic of temporal and spatial scales and coordinates, sometimes subtle and subterfuge, more usually brutal, violent and without redress. They are always global in their intent.

Such considerations throw a very different light into the south of the world and the so-called 'southern question'. Here we discover not pockets of underdevelopment, inhabited by those who apparently live outside the measured pulse of modernity and who have not yet been invested by its progress, but what Gramsci referred to as 'traces of autonomous initiatives'. These signal the multiple contours of the modern world where a hegemonic current is folded into local activity, crossed by translation and mixed by tradition, sounded and sourced in the ongoing construction of place and belonging. The blueprint is both dirtied and deviated, punctuated by the dense grammars of cultural immediacies, by a resistance to a unique will.

What lies 'south of the border' in the seeming excess of life that does not respect the rules, is often seen as a threat to the disciplined productivity of the staged accumulation of capitalist and cultural redemption. These other, southern, spaces, however, are not merely decadent and unruly peripheries, expelled from the motor of modernity. Rather, they propose the challenge of heterotopia. Although constantly seeking to establish borders, set limits, monitor unrest and patrol confines, hegemonic versions of modernity are unable to produce a distinct exterior, a not yet modern or still primitive elsewhere. What is othered, rendered subaltern and subordinate by the institutions and practices of 'advanced' capitalist culture is at the same time structurally integral to the very production and reproduction of dominance and subordination.[16] The negated, feared and despised 'native', black, Jew, Arab, Muslim, Rom, and migrant other is inside the modernity that seeks to define, discipline and decide his or her place. No matter how objectified and anonymously rendered, the subaltern is nevertheless a historical actor, a subjective force *within* a manifold modernity.[17] His or her structural liminality produces a conceptual turbulence at the heart of our reasoning, forcing us to experiment and reconnect the induced fractures. It is this negated conviviality that sets the terms for an unrecognised historical and cultural communality. The chains of power are here tested (and not simply suffered), stretched and sometimes snap. If, then, there is no absolute outside to house the excluded and the damned, there is also no untouched nor pure alternative to the historical network and assemblage in which these political and cultural relations are inscribed. It is precisely in this sense that Gramsci's 'southern question' expands from its initial location in southern Italy to irrupt within the midst of a modernity still to be registered and recognised.

Exemplified in Carlo Levi's *Christ Stopped at Eboli*, Ernesto De Martino's ethnographic field research in the Mezzogiorno of Italy in the 1950s, and the cinema of Pier Paolo Pasolini, seemingly pre-modern practices, beliefs and customs are not 'back there', in an abjured or primitive past, but are 'in here', part of the stratified and subaltern complexities of the present. Their presence renders the familiar un-homely.[18] The present becomes plural and incomplete; that is, irreducible to a single point of view or manner of narration. Along this critical path lies the injunction to think less *of* the south and rather more *with* the south. Here, where historical, cultural, and structural conditions have been formed in subordination to the needs of the north of the world, the inherited critical frame is destabilised. The powerful lessons of the Subaltern Studies group in India, of the lengthy radical tradition of Black Atlantic intellectuals and artists, of the critical constellation of decolonial Latin American thought and practice, all push us in this direction. The abstract universality of 'progress', 'humanism' and 'democracy' comes undone in the cruel insistence of being historically embedded in power, exploitation and unjust cultural detail. This observation, most obviously drawn from Frantz Fanon's *The Wretched of the Earth*, allows us to register the structural inequalities of economic, political, social and cultural justice that characterise the souths of the world while at the same time comprehending their essential role in reproducing the existing powers of the planet.

THE END OF INNOCENCE

In an essay published in 1988 entitled 'New Ethnicities', Stuart Hall announced the end of innocence for the 'essential black subject'.[19] Learning from the complex geography of black identity formations within Occidental modernity it is perhaps also the case to insist even more incisively on the end of innocence for the ubiquitous 'white subject'. This evokes a philosophical challenge to the assumed neutral, hence universal, coordinates for comprehending modernity. Occidental philosophy has rarely responded to this provocation. There is no 'postcolonial philosophy' in the accepted institutional or academic sense of the term. A discursive formation—European philosophy—apparently directly inherited from a tradition that was inaugurated on the shores of the Mediterranean by the Greeks, is here potentially interrupted. It is neither cancelled, ignored, nor simply subverted; rather it is forced to travel in an altogether more extensive space. A *continuity* that is nurtured and guaranteed by questions apparently generated from *within* the autonomous realm of thought is potentially disrupted.

Precisely one of the ways to think the philosophical and cultural impact of cultural and postcolonial studies in the anglophone world would in fact be to consider the fundamental figure of the late Stuart Hall. In the passage from the Caribbean to Europe there lies the entwining of a critical and biographical figure that leads, after empire, to thinking 'without guarantees'; now viewed through the supplementary lenses of race, gender, and ethnicity.[20] This is a worldly location that cannot be ignored or simply separated from critical language. To be a 'black' male, and the object of a 'sound colonial education' (Derek Walcott), is by no means merely an individual trait. It is precisely this dimension—the bio-political location of the voice in a critical cartography profoundly marked by the asymmetrical powers of colonialism—that ignites what has probably acquired the most prominence in the field of cultural and postcolonial studies and its potential impact upon contemporary philosophical configurations: the question of identity. To what degree the insistence of a body located, marked and constructed by race, ethnicity and gender, is allowed to intervene in the fashioning of 'philosophy' is by no means clear. Its ambiguous status disseminates a disturbance, an interrogation.

It is this slightly unruly, even irreverent, appropriation that induces a critical disposition whereby the 'external' and the unrecognised, or 'non-philosophical', irrupts into the field. The body that is referenced at this point is not the abstract entity of Lévinasian alterity that produces an ethical distinction within thought, but the disruptive subject who disturbs thinking precisely with what thinking has failed or refused to contemplate.[21] In this scenario, the postcolonial body—historically marked and culturally located—is not so much a figure that seeks to establish an identity; he or she, as Fanon pointed out many decades ago, has already been thoroughly and sharply subjected to one: 'Look, a Negro!'. He or she is rather a figure that *reveals* the price and power of identity: its mechanisms, its disciplinary modalities, its ideologies. Here, thinking the very grounds of thought, and refusing to 'be' what was previously ordained, takes us elsewhere. The very question of identity (for whom? where, when and how?) becomes problematic for *all*, and not merely for those previously located in the designated marginality and subaltern positions of being black, native, female, queer, indigenous, and other: everything that disturbs the colourless universality of patriarchal whiteness.

At this point it also becomes legitimate to ask whether, for example, Frantz Fanon's *Les damnés de la terre* (1961) should be considered a philosophical text. The very question poses a potential reconfiguration of the philosophical if we are to include it or, conversely, marks a precise institutional exclusion if we ignore it. Fanon's writings most certainly invade and interrupt any thinking that considers itself to be universal and the epitome of humanity. In his Preface to the text, Sartre famously defines Fanon as carrying out a 'strip-tease of our humanism'. It was from such a European universalism that the chilling certainties of racist legislation descended upon the planet. For in the cultural codification of difference only the European is seemingly a moral subject capable of deciding universal values. History in the colonial world is hence exclusively the history of the coloniser and an extension of the European metropolis. The colonised is immobilised, fixed in her subaltern status, and stabilised in the repetition of a cultural identity that is not permitted to disturb the teleological movement of the European coloniser's 'progress'.

This is a complex constellation that while obviously critical is not always obviously philosophical per se; or, rather, it evokes the potential of an interruption and the end of philosophical innocence. Against scholarly security, attention is directed to the performative instance of critical thought. There is the enunciation of a volatile location destined to irritate inherited categories of understanding with an ambivalence that insists on the complexity and opaqueness of the world that thought seeks to frame and render transparent. To insist on what sticks out in language is, as the Indian historian Ranajit Guha forcefully argues in *History at the Limit of World-History*, to deviate and subvert a sequentiality that anticipates its conclusions; it is to snap the chains of *that* history which considers itself to be the unique reason of the world. This is precisely to reintroduce what *that* language has avoided and negated.

To return to Frantz Fanon: for this French-educated Martinican, Europe is not about the fulfilment of humanity, but historically represents the mystification and blocking of its realisation. The West holds humanity in hostage, and humanism is transformed into a hypocrisy that consistently evades a 'humanisme à la mesure du monde' (Césaire 1972). So 'under-development' is not the sign of European superiority but rather an insulting term whose genesis reveals the cruel centrality of colonialism in the making of the modern world: 'L'Europe est littéralement la création du tiers monde' (Fanon 2000). Fixed in the historical vice forged by Europe, the rest of the planet experiences a continual negation of its humanity in the deathly politics that shadow the ex-colonial world.[22] Object of the exception—'Look, a Negro!'—the subaltern is (mis)recognised, her subjectivity erased. She has no other choice than that of shattering the mirror and refusing an imposed alterity. Only in this manner can she abjure the deadly abstraction of being colonised by 'thing-ification', to use Aimé Césaire's term.[23] As the mute and immobile object of Western history she has no alternative but to violate what frames her as an object in order to appropriate the right to narrate. To disrupt an imposed and inherited history is not to evoke a philosophy of violence. Rather it is to reply to the very structures that sustain and disseminate violence; *in primis*, the reign of terror so vividly described by Michael Taussig whereby European colonialism imposes its 'self' on the rest of the world.[24] It is here that we confront the structures of violence, the violence of the structures that cage the colonial and subaltern within modernity itself.

Inevitably, resistance to the legalised violence of colonialism is reduced to 'terrorism'. Just think of the scene in Gillo Pontecorvo's film *The Battle of Algiers* (1966) where the captured National Liberation Front (Front de Libération Nationale [FLN]) leader Larbi Ben M'Hidi is interviewed by French journalists. Asked to explain why the FLN employ women carrying bombs in bags and baskets to explode in the streets and bars of Algiers that kill and wound civilians, he responds by suggesting that these are the only options available unless the colonial power, busy napalming villages from the air, donate tanks and planes to permit a conventional form of warfare. The colonised who refuses to remain in that state have little choice. They are already inserted in a structure of violence. To escape the colonial world requires a forceful wrenching free from its logic. It is not a moral choice taken in a neutral playing field of equal antagonisms as liberal commentary would like to suggest, whether talking of Algeria yesterday or of Palestine today. It is a historical necessity dictated by the overwhelming disparity in power and force produced by the colonial condition. It is not a question of choosing to support Hamas in Gaza, but rather of understanding the colonial production of that situation, where any form of resistance and refusal can only, of necessity, acquire power through the violent insistence to exist and to be. As Fanon taught us, this means to reach critically beyond the existing humanist framework which reduces everything to the abstract morality of 'human beings' precisely at the point where some are considered more 'human' than others (the anonymously colonised and subordinated who are simply natives, blacks, Arabs, Palestinians, and so on).

Bearing Naoki Sakai's earlier words in mind while excavating the archives of modernity, we uncover conditions of thought that are inextricably woven into the making of a world designed to mirror, sanction and extend that very same thought. Even those most directly affected by the rhetoric of the 'progress' and the rule of reason—slaves waging war for their freedom on an eighteenth-century island in the French Caribbean—continue to be excluded from the historical, political, cultural and philosophical account: 'I met History once, but he ain't recognize me' (Derek Walcott).[25] The Jacobins of the Black Atlantic, from Touissant L'Ouverture and the creation of Haiti, to C.L.R. James, Aimé Césaire, Frantz Fanon, James Baldwin, Malcolm X, the Black Panthers, and Stuart Hall, pose a series of burning interrogations that sear both the pages of historical documents and the daily textures of Occidental life. This constitutes a largely unanswered political and philosophical challenge. The historically excluded, the cultural other, the racially abnegated, cannot be absorbed without inducing a sea change in the cartographies of thought (and power). We here return to Fanon's insistence on the necessity to escape the clutches of a history that legitimises the coloniser who continues to narrate the metropolis on the colonial soil that he is stealing.[26] It means to sabotage his historiography and geography; that is, his particular narration of time and space.

It was another Martiniquan, the poet Aimé Césaire, who drew out the terrible equivalence between colonialism and totalitarianism. Once again Fanon reminds his readers of this disturbing vicinity: 'It was my philosophy professor, a native of the Antilles, who recalled the fact to me one day:

'Whenever you hear anyone abuse the Jews, pay attention, because he is talking about you'.[27] As Césaire insisted, the real 'scandal' of Hitler and the Nazi regime was not about a crime against humanity, but a 'crime against the white man, the humiliation of the white man, and the fact that he applied to Europe colonialist procedures which until then had been reserved exclusively for the Arabs of Algeria, the coolies of India, and the blacks of Africa'.[28] These were no longer distant crimes perpetuated on colonial populations, but were directly exercised on the bodies and lives of white, 'civilised' Europeans, selected and segregated according to racial hierarchies that had been perpetuated for centuries overseas. Here the Shoah, and the exceptional concentration of an industrialised genocide, enters another genealogy: that of the long history of colonial terror coming home to be exercised on European soil. In its extreme immediacy, Auschwitz becomes the shocking realisation of the debt of European modernity to colonial reason.[29] As one commentator has recently suggested: 'Césaire takes the camp—to the degree that its exceptional status permits the comprehension of the concentrated colonial universe—as symbolising, to paraphrase Giorgio Agamben's formula, the bio-political *nomos* of colonialism'.[30] We are brought at this point to Albert Memmi's noted affirmation that, in its inescapable structural inequality, every colonial system is a form of fascism. Today, it is impossible not to note how this has reached a paradoxical state in the contemporary politics of Israel. We are forced to recognise, as Hannah Arendt, Primo Levi, and more recently Judith Butler, have courageously argued, that 'precisely from within the moral framework derived from the Holocaust, an opposition to the politics of the Israeli state that produces Palestinian statelessness is not only possible, but necessary'.[31]

Philosophy as an institutional practice, as a discursive field, is historically dependent on the formation of modern Europe, on the persistent distance and differing of the metropolitan centre from the colonial periphery. Yet this framing is consistently betrayed by the political and cultural economy that establishes and identifies centre and periphery, First and Third worlds, developed and underdeveloped. For the very sense of Europe, its authority and reason, is dependent, as the Congolese philosopher Valentin Y. Mudimbe has carefully argued, on the existence and invention of Africa, Asia, Oceania, and the Americas. Breaking the 'implacable dependence' (Albert Memmi) between the coloniser and the colonised, it becomes impossible to ignore a fracture destined to vibrate throughout the body of Occidental thought; its abstract purity stained by the contingent disruptions of unruly histories, undisciplined knowledges, negated bodies and the brutal inscriptions of power. To think, to philosophise, in such a historical constellation—whether acknowledged or not—is clearly to unchain thought from its earlier anchorage in a Western harbour. It is to push it out to navigate in altogether wider and more worldly currents. Here the repressed colonial archive, and hence the secret histories of the historical and cultural making of modernity and its overall political economy, can no longer be evaded or ignored.

It is at this point that with Gayatri Chakravorty Spivak we can ask who is the 'we' of philosophy? In her extended discussion of the anthropological moment of Kantian reason in the context of *The Critique of Pure Reason* (1781), the Bengali critic points to the philosopher's evocation of the non-European native as the limit case of reason: 'He is only a *casual* object of thought, not a paradigmatic example. He is not only not the subject as such; he also does not quite make it as an example of the thing or its species as natural product'. In other words, the presence of the native of Tierra del Fuego or the Australian Aboriginal is not required, need not even exist, for the passage of philosophy to occur. Such 'natives' sustain a narrative—anthropological, instances of the exotic and the sublime—that does not yet bear the European signature of history. As the author of *A Critique of Postcolonial Reason* (the very title announces a doubling and dispersal of the inherited imposition of Kantian thought) concludes: 'We find here the axiomatics of imperialism as a natural argument to indicate the limits of the cognition of (cultural) man. . . . The subject as such in Kant is geopolitically differentiated'. [32]

The reply here is most certainly not about how to appropriate the 'native informant' in order to mend and propose a reconfigured discourse—yet a further colonial move—but precisely to leave the gaps, the holes, in critical language open, susceptible to eventual suturing into another place, another language, another subject-hood. Here lies the nucleus of a question that threatens to challenge Western philosophy with radically unsuspected conditions. More than two centuries after Kant, the provenance of the pronouncement continues to configure the analytical constellation in a 'topographical re-inscription of imperialism' that invariably, even in its most radical formulations, exposes First World concerns. [33] Via an intellectually staged ventriloquism, the rest of the world is still reduced to the rules of representation that reaffirm the philosopher's will. Subjected to the totalising maps of the *power* and *desire* of political and ideological representation, there is a simultaneous disavowal of the asymmetrical, inconclusive and lived complexities of other, worldly subjects.

The failure and refusal to track discontinuity—geographical, political, social, and cultural—in the differentiated but entwined complexity of what is clearly now a planetary mode of production and becoming continues to ensure the sovereignty of the Occidental subject as *the* subject of history. The point that Spivak is making here is that the subaltern is not allowed to invest in her own itinerary. She, like Fanon's 'Negro', is already produced and spoken for in a logic over-determined by an existing political economy and associated cultural configurations. The eventual rent and discontinuity in this discursive tissue necessarily challenges the sanctioned ignorance of a simulated identification with the 'other', which is always about some form of self-investment. For the discontinuous registers precisely what exceeds and escapes 'my' world as an insistent irreducibility: a perpetual interrogation and interruption of my 'self' and its associated languages of meaning and managing the world.

THE SELLING OF THE PLANET

The mounting militarisation of modern society, from security agendas, policing procedures and border controls to the instalment of the military as a civil authority and political power, is an integral part of the present-day neoliberal economy. What is experienced today as the harsh economic and political disciplining of populations in the northern hemisphere has been elaborated (and resisted) in the rest of the world for more than forty years. Inaugurated in Chile with the U.S.-backed overthrow of the democratically elected Allende government and the imposition of Chicago School economics by General Pinochet in 1973, neoliberalism under the aegis of the International Monetary Fund and the World Bank has consistently dominated the so-called south of the world, both in Africa and Latin America. In an altogether more recent context, one can speak of an archipelago of refusals, revolts and rebellions to that order that stretches from Latin America to the eastern Mediterranean, from Tahrir to Taksim Square, from Buenos Aires to Tunis, Cairo and Madrid (with briefer flashes in London and New York). That the fallout of this social unrest is not politically guaranteed is clear, but equally certain is that these fractures and frictions are destined to continue.

Devolving social responsibility on the citizen, or else denying the status of the individual to appear as such (for example, the clandestine body of the 'illegal' migrant), the present-day state configures the very productivity of the 'self' to advance the impersonal laws of the market. How we individually labour in the present configuration of the political economy reproduces a political asset that assures the extraction of capital rather than the promotion and protection of society.[34] Politics in the West has unequivocally shifted to adopting the brutal clarity of this mandate and abandoned the unstable equations of social justice. As the rich get richer and the poor grow in number, capital carves an ever deeper wound into the body of the world: from dispossessed multitudes, to ecological breakdown and species extinction. The violence of the extraction, logistics, and management of it all is augmented by the supplement of an ecological dimension whose belated recognition cuts ever more dramatically into the normative premises of this political economy. Meanwhile, the continuum of crisis becomes the operative modality for managing economic extraction, financial flows, social inequality and the politics of an expanding precarious condition.

In this transfiguration of the earlier liberal state there emerges the systematic abolition of the very idea of alienation as the individual subject and the market economy become one: work is no longer about exploitation and labour but is rather about the productive creation of one's individuality. Government, too, is less about an external apparatus supervising social development and increasingly more about promoting the passage of responsibility, management and care to the 'self'.[35] We move from a heterogeneous construction of the subject—drawing on multiple and even conflictual sources of identity reflected in a diversity of institutions and moral, intellectual, economic, political, and cultural norms—to a homogeneous one that is to be measured and verified in the seeming transparency offered by the quantitative world of the market. With the reduction of politics to the authority of the coordinated economies of the self, the media and censorship acquire a different form. Self-government flows through the bio-politicised body into a media-induced 'common sense' whose actors activate auto-censorship: there is no alternative, this is reality—other versions, visions and interpretations fall off the screen. This is to concur with Michel Foucault that at this point governmentality and the care of the self become one. Each becomes interlocked in the other as the personal and the political come to be measured solely in terms of success or failure. It is now this manner of acknowledged reasoning, certainly not the critical language of historical responsibility and cultural accountability, that has come to be naturalised as the normative, as the regime of truth. If such a scenario prepares the premises for mandated authoritarian rule it is not seamless. In exploring its fissures, cracks, and misfits we come upon a critical space in which understanding the networked mobility of a shifting topology of powers invites us precisely to reconsider modalities of hegemony and subject formations, both locally and trans-nationally.

Here we also need to register the increasing difficulty of separating out the present cresting of neoliberalism from the altogether longer wave of the complex formation of European liberalism. There are continuities and discontinuities; but there *are* continuities. To unpack the moral economy of contemporary neoliberalism is inevitably to be drawn back into an altogether older archive in which the hierarchical organisation and exploitation of the world through the liberal ideology of protecting and expanding property rights was, and remains, central. In this sense, liberalism and neoliberalism do not form opposite poles. They are accented differently, and deploy diverse cultural and political lexicons and resources. If it is no longer the state that arbitrates the market but the market itself that dictates the programs and policies of the state, we are still within the spectrum and shifting dynamics of the political economy promoted by classical liberalism.

The precise shift in emphasis, but not the break, lies in the political rationality of government whereby the modern individual is embedded in what Thomas Lemke calls the 'universalization of the entrepreneurial form' and its extension 'to the social sphere, thus eliding any difference between the economy and the social'.[36] We are forced to adopt the modality of becoming entrepreneurs of our selves. The public is privatised and we are returned to the bottom line of individual responsibility for our education, health, well-being, and prosperity. Motored by fictitious wealth and financial wizardry, serviced by credit and debt, this is the landscape in which the struggle for historical change, attuned to democratic possibilities and the emergent scenarios, occurs. The shift from liberalism to neoliberalism is here most sharply marked in the collapsing of distinctions between the domains of the economy, the juridical, the political, and the cultural: all is now to be evaluated and rendered transparent in terms of competitive criteria and market performance. In this line of argument, education and the arts are expected to be advancing this situation, certainly not contesting it. Capital and culture become one.[37] In this vein the distinction between public and private evaporates. It leads to a profound alteration in political and cultural practices, a significant change in the very understanding of what constitutes social and cultural goals, and a sharp break from any idea of collective welfare or well-being. This is a political settlement, as Chantal Mouffe has pointed out, that cannot accommodate contradiction or antagonism.[38] To ensure its continuing hegemony the rules of consensus are increasingly removed from the public eye, secured in the back office of government and secret international trade agreements protecting corporate capital. At this point giant pharmaceutical companies can successfully lobby against improving health standards that would threaten the profits of their existing products.

In August 2012 the South African police killed thirty-four miners at Marikana near Johannesburg. As a protest for a wage rise that a London-based mining company was unwilling to grant in order not to cut into profits and shareholders' dividends this reminds us of the actuality of the struggle between labour and capital within a globalised world. Thomas Piketty, from whom I draw this example from South Africa, and who is certainly no Marxist, suggests that the violent struggle between capital and labour, associated in Europe with a past epoch, is destined to return. It will be accompanied by the reduction of the vast part of the world's population to economic and political servitude. Recently it has been estimated that just over 100 companies, most of them British, own more than $800 billion worth of platinum, oil and coal in Africa. Meanwhile, the continent loses around $80 billion a year through tax avoidance and the profits extracted by multinational companies traveling elsewhere.[39] Once the parenthesis of social democracy (1945–1975) is stripped away it is back to the basic drives of capitalist accumulation, accompanied by the continuing colonial carve-up of the world. Today, and in a further turn of the screw, the profits harvested by financial capital on the global market now far outstrip those coming from the growth of production and rent. Miguel Etchevehere, president of the *Sociedad Rural* in Argentina, recently put it like this: 'rather than produce it is better to speculate'. It is better to keep silos full of soya as a chip to play in international financial exchange rather than sell it in the alimentary market.[40] The power of labour as an exchangeable commodity is both further marginalised and altogether more ferociously disciplined. In this manner, capitalism produces an accelerating inequality. Liberal values ensconced in free market fundamentalism radically undo the vaunted values of meritocracy as the foundation of a democratic society.[41] The resultant state of hypocrisy is invariably run by oligarchies and their political cronies.

The multiplication of social actors and processes today poses a new set of scenarios. Not only has the unitary referent of class been complicated by the planetary reorganisation of labour through diversification and multiplication, but the cultural insistence of social formations that secure a sense of belonging in gender, sexuality, religion, race and ethnicity have become intractable elements in renegotiating the political and historical sense of the present and the future. As Pierre Dardot has recently argued, capitalism is irreducible to a mode of production or the mechanisms of the market and the economy. It is now clearly a juridical-economic-political-cultural complex. It is, as Marx insisted, a political economy, whose direction, as Gramsci argued, involves the struggle for political and cultural hegemony. Today its governance is characterised by the promotion of competition, enforced by juridical means, to create a mobile entrepreneurism that configures society and the individual through the extension of the market rationale to the multiple intricacies inscribed in subjectivity itself.[42]

OTHER MAPS, OTHER SPACES, OTHER PLACES

Dipesh Chakrabarty's noted 'provincializing of Europe' invites us to relocate the previous discussion at a global level. This is to emphasise the geography of power in the intent of maps, the scale of their pertinence, their figuration of resources and measurement of influence. In their exploration of this geography, Antonio Gramsci and Edward Said consistently confronted how the world is shaped and configured in the struggle between hegemonic mappings and those who resist, refuse, and reroute that cartography. If this promotes a postcolonial mapping of the world, one traced from below and elsewhere, it also sustains the challenge of proximity: what Sandro Mezzadra and Brett Neilson refer to as the implosion of previously distinct territories and subjects.[43] Refusals, resistances, and responses now occur within the communal space of a differentiated modernity. The arguments being made here seek to register the contemporary significance and critical weight of such responses.

When considered from within the heartlands of the Occident, such previously marginalised forms and subaltern forces propose the collective global specificity of what could be called a translated modernity. Again drawing upon Gramsci's understanding of the complex and fluid making of cultural formations, while listening to the precise arguments elaborated more recently by Naoki Sakai, this is to insist on the translating and translatable qualities of a modernity that does not simply find its source or definition in the West.[44]

At this point the modern European nation state as the 'natural' home of the historical narrative begins to fall apart. A particular knowledge production is uncoupled from a single site of authorisation, whether that be disciplinary or geographical. This means, as Sakai points out, to insist on the transnationalism that always shadows and sustains the cultural and historical transit of translation. Sakai's advice, which I am following here, is to commence from that excess or surplus that permits the initial drawing of a boundary and a border, and which permits the distinction (national, disciplinary) to emerge. As I have argued elsewhere, it is frankly impossible to conceive of the historical and cultural formation of the modern Mediterranean, for example, through the mere addition of one national narrative to another.[45] There is an instructive surplus involved that lies beyond such limits. Similarly, the national formation of knowledge is not simply provincial in its grasp of the matter; it is also marked by an epistemic blindness inherited from the history of its localism. What we today consider to be the national is the repressed and unacknowledged outcome of Edward Said's famous 'overlapping territories and intertwined histories'.[46] Here we discover that the local and 'traditional' have never been fully circumscribed by immediate understandings of identity and homeland. As James Clifford recently reminds us, 'the very idea of history is kept in quotation marks, suspended in relations of translation'.[47] Here not only borders but also 'ambivalence becomes a kind of method'.[48]

While seemingly so central to the narrative that we tell ourselves we are slowly uncovering a neurosis that negates its sickness. Buried under biographies, autobiographies, and narratives secured in the progress of capital and culture, we in the West are continually obsessed with histories that negate history. Captured in empirical detail, or in the idealism of metaphysical constructs, the challenge of history as a constellation of planetary processes constantly composing and recomposing past, present and future is squashed beneath our self-obsessions. The hysteria of history that calls itself the West, is the hegemonic version of modernity, progress and democracy that understands itself to be providing the unique and universal narrative of the world: a paradoxically atemporal template. Beyond that empire of sense lies the challenge of what does not necessarily follow its beat and respond to its rhythms. This is not only to talk of the negated other, Fanon's wretched of the earth, and conjure up the historical, cultural, and political challenge of the postcolonial world. It also means to operate a profound cut on the body and corpus of

Occidental knowledge and its manner of framing the resources and responses of the planet. Beyond the desire for a dialectical overturning of the existing order lies an altogether more radical reconfiguration that touches us all, both in the West and the rest of the world.

ART AND BEYOND

This proposed cut can acquire different languages and modalities. Those elaborated in the critique of political economy are the most noted. To insist, as in what follows, on the cultural and historical textures of this economy is not to contrast capital with culture. Rather, it is to seek to deepen the lived sense of a historical formation in which capital and culture have become indistinguishable, and there to register its limits in a world that exceeds its claims. Attentive to the ethical horizons sustained in the aesthetics of sound and vision, in musics and the visual arts in particular, I will try to make an argument about the political import of poetics that participates in the critical reconfiguration of the world we have inherited. This is to not to talk of the universal aesthetics that the Occident has historically promoted, but is rather to consider the universality of the political economy that has produced the historical and cultural conditions of the postcolonial world. Thinking with music and the visual arts is not simply to seek an alternative catalogue of subaltern and subversive replies to Western hegemony. It is also to consider instances of art working the elaboration of counter-intuitive critical spaces. Seeing and sounding modernity in a different key is to cut up and disperse a unilateral framing of the world.

If the art works discussed in this volume indicate what Deleuze and Guattari would have called lines of flight they also provoke spaces from where it becomes possible to renegotiate a critical relationship to a modernity lived and figured otherwise. For the sounds and signs considered are not merely the historical testimony of alternative understandings and critical refusals of the status quo. They themselves are instances of critical languages that impact directly on our understanding of the possibilities and potentialities of a modernity freed from a single source of legitimation. We are encouraged to consider them less as objects of art, history, and culture and more to think *with* them as instigators of critical practices. From aesthetic instances of the political economy of the present, such works, drawing upon a postcolonial cartography of time and space, provoke processes that unsettle the existing framing of art and aesthetics. Their poetics disseminate the disturbance of another politics.

In this attempt to sketch counter-atlases of modernity, ones that commence from considering the so-called periphery and south of the world, there is no wish to propose a simple counter-image. Rather, in the resonance between diverse instances of subaltern, repressed, and renounced histories, the following prospects seek to follow a critical itinerary that responds to a world still to be mapped and registered. This means to tilt the axis and establish a perspective that while unable to cancel inherited prospectives begins to view them anew, in an oblique manner, proposing diverse passages across a terrain that we think we already know.

Here points of departure that carry multiple names—home, identity, the nation, citizenship, democracy, the West, but also the disciplinary place holders of history, sociology, art—are destined, if not to be abandoned, to be dispersed in a passage that will always exceed their conceptual grasp. Lived as ruins, the languages that previously conceived and explained our world disband to be worked into critical narratives that are open, incomplete, still in the making. The linearity of a presumed progress breaks down. The past irrupts in the present, the repressed returns and shards of time co-exist, just as colonialism and Euro-American civil society co-existed and continue to co-exist. Knowledge is neither single nor complete. It is imbricated in a planetary ecology. As Maurice Merleau-Ponty once argued, we move from the precise European custody and imperial capture of an overarching 'universal' towards the lateral details and specificities of a shared 'universality' that is ultimately irreducible to a single framing, authority or explanation. It is here that we can begin to separate out the European humanism peddled by colonial powers from altogether more radical understandings proposed by Frantz Fanon and Paul Gilroy. Souleymane Bachir Diagne, from whom I draw the Merleau-Ponty reference, argues that the postcolonial world we inhabit necessarily involves a criticism of a particular conception of the universal in the name of a universality that is not simply a homage to Europe.[49] Evoked in multiple sites the latter understanding brings us through both differences and commonalities to worlds exposed, relayed, and reworked in unacknowledged translation. Slave revolts in the Caribbean and North America, as with indigenous resistance and subaltern rebellion, were precisely instances of a universality seeking a freedom that exceeded its confinement in the hands of white legislators and *their* interpretation of 'universal' values. The universality proposed here has neither a single source, nor is it waiting to be emancipated by the West.[50]

In more immediate terms, this also means to confront the evidence that the colonial modality of violently appropriating the world is most clearly not back there, now safely locked up in the annals of the past. We only need to think of the continuous privatisation of nature in the form of contemporary land grabbing and patent poaching, wars in the Congo for primary materials essential for cell phone production, the global organisation of agriculture and resources for First World needs, the infinite practices of violent appropriation pursued by Israel in Palestine, the racist discrimination and exploitation of labour and lives everywhere. These are the violent hierarchies established by capitalism in the formation of Euro-American modernity, today globalised via neoliberal protocols, that deliberately ignore an altogether wider world in the pursuit of its own well-being, freedom, and security. This is colonialism. It is also the poisoned historical fruit of liberalism that justified the global extension of European government, genocide, slavery, and apartheid.[51] Both are historically and culturally essential to the political economy of the present.

It is in this context, and returning to the complex entwining of capital and culture, that another poetics can be continually posed. This is to propose thinking with art that is spliced into a postcolonial aesthetics in a manner that permits an exit from being held hostage in the limited humanism of the West. In place of the consolation of the bodiless sense of the beautiful that reconfirms the subject in her language and domestic surroundings there here exists a deliberate sabotage that provokes a disquieting unsettlement. The work that mirrors our desires and directives in the seeming transparency of language is dirtied and displaced. The surface of both the artistic object and the receiving body is creased and folded by what precedes and exceeds their meeting. It is a matter irreducible to the abstract geometry of the encounter. It suggests an aesthetics and 'realism' that muddies and misplaces the mimetic. For the matter in question, the materiality that composes the event is neither simply human nor restricted to the placid multiplication of modernity.

Laying to rest the conceptual unity of thought embodied in the singular reflection of history and culture is to undo the unilateralism of our understanding of the universal. It means to touch the rougher ground of an altogether more extensive and dynamic universality that involves other lives and processes, both human and non. We move in a terrestrial landscape, not only differentiated by histories and cultures, but also by what we call 'nature'. The latter is neither still, dumb nor dead. So the postcolonial tear in the tissue of Occidental humanism opens a door on to a far wider vista in which we come to discover ourselves to be subjected to temporal processes and material forces that flow through and beyond the human condition.[52] This returns us in the very body of our thought and lives to directly confront the Occidental 'incomprehension of any ontological and ethic structure that is not rooted in the epistemic subject of humanism'.[53] Unable to fully appropriate the situation, whether in the singularity of other bodies and lives, or in the complex materialities of the world at large, a very different 'humanism' is called for. If we wish to hold on to such a term, it becomes an altogether more humble signal for disseminating a necessary recognition of complexity and limits. Marked by its history in the West, extended elsewhere through the exposure of its hypocrisies, for example by Frantz Fanon and James Baldwin, European humanism can no longer guarantee the appropriation of the universal. It can now only serve to promote a responsibility and an apprenticeship; that is, a training and education in a world that is not only ours to administer and define.

It is precisely here that the workings of postcolonial art not only sow an interrogation and interruption in the preceding European-derived order, but also crease our inherent cartographies, exploring the folds of what is visible but rarely seen or registered. In this ethnographic aesthetics, predicted by George Marcus and Fred Myers in 1995, art becomes anthropology.[54] This is where thinking with art as a process and practice, rather than as an object, draws us into another space. Here, we find ourselves on the cusp between humanity and what simultaneously exceeds and supports its claims on the world. For in this deliberate dislocation, the very materiality of memory—the means whereby the future is expectantly framed and figured—turns out to be a migratory assemblage, composed, recomposed and decomposed not only in our bodies, but also in the mineral, vegetable, maritime, molecular and animal life that surrounds and sustains us. That ecological framing is history too.

NOTES

1. Arendt 1973.
2. Balibar 2014.
3. See Agamben 2000.
4. Sakai 2011.
5. Mezzadra and Neilson 2013.
6. The following considerations draw directly from Domenico Losurdo's detailed historical exposition of modern liberalism in Losurdo 2014.
7. Dardot and Laval 2013; see also Holston and Appadurai 1996, 192.
8. Terranova 2009.
9. Baldwin 1963,16.
10. Thompson 2013; Hay et al. 2011.
11. For an excellent overview of the history of enclosure in Britain in the context of the global commons, see Fairlie 2007.
12. Hall, McClelland, Draper, Donington and Lang 2014.
13. Marino 2015.
14. Federici 2004.
15. Sanyal 2007.
16. Mezzadra 2011.
17. Guha 2003.
18. This is also explored in Ernst Bloch's *Heritage of Our Times* (2009), and is inscribed directly in the montage structure of the book itself.
19. Hall 1988.
20. For an audiovisual version of this journey, see Akomfrah 2013.
21. One could fruitfully insert the whole critical oeuvre of Judith Butler into the discussion at this point.
22. Mbembe 2013°.
23. Césaire 1972, 6.
24. Taussig 1991.
25. Walcott 1992.
26. Fanon 2004.
27. Fanon 1986.

28. Césaire 1972, 3.
29. Bauman 1991.
30. Costantini 2006, 218.
31. Butler 2004. Primo Levi in Belpoliti and Gordon 2001. On Primo Levi, see also Perugini and Zucconi 2012. On Hannah Arendt, see Butler 2007.
32. Spivak 1999, 26–27. See also Park 2013.
33. Spivak 1999, 279.
34. Hardt and Mezzadra, 2015.
35. Dardot and Laval 2013.
36. Lemke 2001, 195, 197.
37. Davies 2014.
38. Mouffe 2000.
39. Curtis 2016.
40. Tognonato 2014.
41. Piketty 2014.
42. Dardot 2013.
43. Mezzadra and Neilson 2013.
44. Sakai 2011.
45. Chambers 2008.
46. Said 1994.
47. Clifford 2013, 15.
48. Clifford 2013, 18.
49. Diagne 2013.
50. Mignolo 2010, 321.
51. Losurdo 2014.
52. Chakrabarty 2009.
53. Iuliano 2012, 157.
54. Marcus and Myers 1995.

Chapter Four

Lessons from the South

Viewed from London, Los Angeles, New York, Berlin, Paris, and Milan, the south of the world is invariably considered in terms of lacks and absences. It is not yet modern, it has still to catch up. It remains, as Dipesh Chakrabarty would put it, an inadequate place.[1] The south is spatially and temporally located elsewhere, at the edge of the map. Of course, as we know from Edward Said, and through him from Antonio Gramsci, this is a geography of power. It is about being placed and systematised in a manner not of your own choosing. It is also about being rendered subordinate and subaltern to other forces, and being exploited, not only economically, but also politically and culturally, in order for that subaltern position to be reproduced and reinforced. The south of the world is persistently framed: not only conceptually enclosed, but also falsely accused of failing to respect and achieve a modernity being triumphantly pursued elsewhere.

To return to the south as a critical, political, and historical problem is, as we have seen, ultimately to return to the north and its hegemonic management of the planet. The ills, failures, and breakdowns that are located down there, across the border, are precisely the products of a northern will to make the world over in its image and interests. This is the political economy of location, and the dark underbelly of the global formation of the modern world. Here the multiple souths, of Italy, of Europe, of the Mediterranean, of the globe, are rendered both marginal but paradoxically central to the reproduction of that economy. If the whole world were equally modern then the competitive logic that divides and drives modernity would collapse. The cancellation of inequalities, property, and differences that charge the planetary circuits of capitalist accumulation would render the concept superfluous. As James Baldwin captured it: 'it is not even remotely possible for the excluded to become included, for this inclusion means, precisely, the end of the *status quo*—or would result, as so many of the wise and honored would put it, in a mongrelization of the races'.[2] The subversion of this hierarchal and racial accounting of 'progress' undoes historical time as it is presently understood. For the 'south' as a political and historical question is, above all, about the power exercised on those held in its definitions. It is at this point, slipping back in time to the fourteenth century, we can grasp the profounder sense of the historiographical operation through listening to the words of Ibn Khaldûn:

> The inner meaning of history . . . involves speculation and an attempt to get at the truth, subtle explanation of the causes and origins of existing things, and deep knowledge of the how and why of events. History, therefore is firmly rooted in philosophy.[3]

ELECTRIC AVENUE

On the street at night: it is warm but not too humid. Nairobi is over 1600 metres above sea level. We're strolling on Electric Avenue in the Westlands district. This is the heart of Nairobi club land. The volume is incredible. Even walking in the open it is impossible to converse. This is musical warfare. Between cars and pedestrians, sounds battle each other seeking their auditory claim on the territory. We stop to take a beer outside on the sidewalk while music bellows out of an open door leading down some steps into a sonorous density so thick as to reverberate through the body, denuded of words or explanation.

Is this a different or an emergent public sphere? It is certainly the active formation of a discursive space.[4] We could even suggest that a form of citizenship, that is perhaps elsewhere formally denied or truncated, is here publicly sustained in sound. Such transitory geographies of musical belonging connect us to the altogether more complex unfolding of the immediacies of the world. We are drawn into multiple temporalities and spaces that link us to what we can rarely fully comprehend or attest to. This takes us beyond the rational conversation that apparently typified the eighteenth-century coffee house and the measured prose of the modern press promoting public debate proposed by Jürgen Habermas.[5] That particular sense of the public sphere, and associated model of citizenship, is contaminated and remixed down here in sub-Saharan Africa (and certainly not only there). In the diverse urban spaces of Nairobi, Naples, Lagos, Lisbon, Luanda, Kiev, Johannesburg, Berlin, Bristol and Cairo, public space is lived, moulded and reconfigured in an ongoing set of practices that scratch, bend, and splinter the presumed model of European provenance, rendering explicit the problematic relationship between citizenship, social space, everyday culture and democracy.[6] Here, European and extra-European scenarios are unsuspectedly conjoined in a 'general questing for democratic agency in an era of declining electoral participation, compromised sovereignties, and frustrated or disappointed citizenship'.[7] Caribbean and Turkish diasporas in Bristol and Berlin, illegal immigrants in the backstreets of Naples, rapping in Arabic, further underline that other versions of public life, citizenship and modernity are at work. Sharp distinctions between public and private life come undone. Just as in Kenya where everything is modern—both the ubiquitous cell phone and the poverty, the midnight car wash in the club complex and the urban slum—a potential democratic participation lies alongside and often independent of the formal manifestations of public politics. In noisily taking the lid of the institutional can, the contents of modernity that can be observed and seen in a Nairobi night invite us to reconsider our lexicon, uncoil our certainties, and take a further walk in the world.

After all, the democracy and citizenship that we claim in the West, fully depends—in both its economic structures and cultural tissues—on the subordination and exclusion of the bodies and histories of those who inhabited the colonial world and who now live in the postcolony. Not only has our 'freedom' been structurally dependent on the extension of non-freedoms (slavery, indenture, genocide) elsewhere, but the liberal formation of modern, European democracy on both sides of the Atlantic is riddled with the perversities of power and property that makes its citizens the bearers of planetary injustice. The rule of law, that is the universal claims of a property-owning class and its political economy to legislate for the world, not only reveals the arbitrary and unilateral powers of a European derived sovereign will on the planet. It also exposes that very same logic to both translation and treason. Elsewhere *within* modernity, the terms of the modern polity are not merely a sham to be wielded by dictators and oligarchs while pursuing their own particular interests. Ideas about citizenship, democracy and the public sphere are everywhere taken up and embodied by subjects engaged in the multiple languages of modernity. In particular, in the immediacies of the simultaneously local and trans-national spaces of the city, lives, cultures, and prospects are both inhabited and appropriated. Time is technologically coordinated in mobile circuitry, DJ mixes, satellite connections, social networks. Traditions are transmitted, transformed, translated. All of this is part of what David Featherstone calls the 'geographies of subaltern connection'.[8]

THE STREETS OF CAIRO

We are now informed by Western experts that the Arab Spring of 2011 did not arrive at a revolutionary stage, even though many blithely refer to the present situation in North Africa and the Middle East as being counter-revolutionary. The model of 1776, 1789, 1848, 1917, has been set, the necessary stages and temporalities understood, the standard established. However, all these earlier revolutions, in one way or another, were also accompanied by a failure in their ideals and their subsequent undoing in counter-revolutions. Their histories draw us into lengthier time scales of evaluation: from the establishment of a white supremacist polity in the United States, to Bonapartism in France, and Stalinism in Soviet Russia. In a critical interruption of conventional chronologies and conceptual verdicts we might, borrowing from the queer theorist Elizabeth Freeman, consider such events, practices and experiences in terms which 'embrace the afterlife of [a series of failed] revolutions as part of the political present tense'.[9] For whatever the immediate outcome, it is also undeniable that they shifted the course and conception of subsequent historical processes. Surely the ready verdict we seek to apply to the Arab Spring is an insult to those involved in the events in North Africa. They are apparently expected to bear the burden of European definitions. Such an act disposes the non-European world of autonomous political initiatives. It conserves the conceptual hegemony of the West and ignores the long unfolding of 'the revolutionary modern history of the region'.[10] The outcome is that colonisation is doubled: both in terms of the Occidental verdict on the 'failure' of the Arab Spring, and in continuing to provide the seemingly unique historical and political benchmark.

This registers the limits of a political semantics that can only reason in the geopolitical lexicon provided by the modern history of Europe, as though that is the categorical history of the world. On the contrary, what becomes most significant here is to consider the 'practices of freedom that "disturbed" and broke the spatial and geopolitical stability of the Mediterranean'.[11] As Martina Tazzioli has argued, in the complex interplay between ongoing migrations and revolutionary uprisings political perspectives on the northern shore are rendered vulnerable and interrogated. The conceptual framework is challenged. A Western political order whose cultural and intellectual violence insists on a unique model of democracy—increasingly dependent on non-accountable governance imposed in the name of security—begins to unravel. What occurred in North Africa were not necessarily 'liberal revolutions' inaugurating the transit to the Occidental polity. Rather, they were also revolts against the Occidental polity that has consistently supported dictatorial regimes in order to ensure political and economic stability in the area. Rebellion on the streets and in the squares was clearly against the immediate grip of despotic government. Yet it also touched a deeper, structural, level as a rebellion against the agendas and policies of 'liberal' Western governance: brokered through the structural adjustment programs of the International Monetary Fund and the World Bank, and imposed through the machinery of the local authoritarian state. The political power of unauthorised and unruly collectives, the 'moral economy of the crowd' composed of fragile, transitory political subjects, has produced rents in the discursive regime that believes itself capable of explaining the crisis in political hegemony.[12] What was involved was more than an attempted 'transition' to 'the liberal utopian narrative of global democratization'; for what occurred in Egypt and elsewhere in the Middle East cannot be divorced from the global relations of power that have consistently sought to define and displace popular revolt and social change.[13]

In fact, the Arab word for revolution—*Al-Thawra*—does not follow the trajectory of failed liberal ideas, but is deeply entrenched in the semantic field of anti-colonial struggle.[14] The idea that there can be an Islamic radicalism, breaking with the revolutionary model of a Western order and leading in all sorts of directions (just as the slave revolt in Haiti necessarily uncoupled itself from Paris 1789 in order to deepen its revolutionary imperative) is perhaps something that the West is not willing to comprehend. This is what in his enthusiastic reporting on the Iranian revolution for *Corriere della Sera* in 1978, Foucault with foresight identified as the powder keg called Islam: 'which is not simply a religion, but an entire way of life, an adherence to a history and a civilisation'.[15] The successful anti-imperialist seizure of power in Tehran—leading for the moment to a clerical regime—perhaps ghosts the contemporary political picture of the Middle East in a far deeper manner than Occidental observers may wish to acknowledge. A moral order in political command, however critical we may be of its contemporary practices, is destined to haunt the hypocrisies of the Christian formation of Occidental polity where ethics have increasingly been expunged from the utilitarian government of a capitalist order. However disquieting it may appear, this draws us to considering a counter project: "that aims to find a moral space for the Muslim subject in the modern world, a subject who has grown no less disenchanted by modernity than his or her Western counterpart. The retrieval of Islamic moral resources is therefore as much a modern project as modernity itself."[16]

In 2011, beneath the media labels, there were deeper struggles already in play: against poverty, structural unemployment, crony capitalism, and the authoritarian negation of political rights in a region profoundly marked for over two centuries by the instabilities, military occupations, and wars induced by the West. The fundamental cry that fuelled the explosion on the streets was '"*Al-sha'b*". Stop. "*Yurid*". Stop. "*Isqat al-Nizam*". Stop. "The people". "Demand". "The downfall of the regime"'.[17] What interests me here, however, is less about getting the analysis right or defining the 'people', and rather more about registering, in the riotous mishmash of demands and ideals, the breaches and uncertainties these events produced amongst those who felt authorised to define and explain the situation.

When mass protests and regime changes swept across North Africa in the spring of 2011, and subsequently triggered turbulence in Bahrain and a bloody and interminable civil war in Syria, Occidental journalism and political commentary was initially taken by surprise. The status quo—and not only for Arab dictators—had seemingly crumbled overnight. The situation was eventually framed and brought under Western eyes through a series of explanatory motives—educated unemployed youth, the new social media, state oppression and the lack of democracy—that responded to the Occidental criteria of analysis. Of course, in conditions of planetary modernity all is somehow connected, nothing takes place in a vacuum, and the languages, technologies and ideologies of the West clearly play a significant role. However, rather than measure such events—their perceived achievements and failures—against a presumed Occidental template it is perhaps politically and historically more significant to register the emergence of a series of interrogations that invest both the immediate protagonists and those of us observing from afar. It might also be important at this point to acknowledge that the processes and procedures under discussion are still very much in progress: the question of rights and liberties—social, political, cultural, historical—remain open, the subject of discussion, debate, and continuing definition and struggle. A previous political landscape, which had been thoroughly endorsed by Western powers and diplomacy, is clearly in ruins. The assumption that only the Occidental 'we' has the right to define freedom and democracy has now been rendered vulnerable to unsuspected historical relations and cultural forces. As Anthony Alessandrini has suggested in the on-line journal *Jadaliyya*:

> In short, the great lesson that Foucault and Fanon have to teach those of us working to understand the unfolding revolutions of North Africa is simply: revolutions change things, and among the things that they change, or should change, are the categories through which we view such changes. New subjectivities and new singularities demand new frameworks, both of understanding and of solidarity.[18]

Emerging from this picture are critical prospects that criss-cross the Mediterranean and the subaltern south, rendering proximate its northern and southern shores, shredding the confines between Occident and Orient. When the terms of political, historical and cultural freedom are exposed—for whom, where, when and how?—a whole critical lexicon comes under review. The assumed temporality of political and historical progress, the accumulative power of its linear regime, is skewed into another space in which modernity is clearly neither mono-dimensional nor homogeneous. The downfall of Mubarak, the daily protests in Tahrir Square, were not simply Egyptian matters. Their resonance was not restricted merely to the Arab world. A political lexicon that many consider to be complete and fully achieved in the governing bodies and institutional authorities of the West has been reopened and freshly traversed and translated. Understandings of the individual, the public sphere, political agency, religion, secularism and the state, suddenly become vulnerable to renegotiation in events and historical formations that rudely punctuate flawless abstractions. This is not to deny the existence of internal debate and critique around these terms within Western intellectual circles; after all, this is historically what cultural and postcolonial studies, or critical anthropology and sociology, have been about. However, these voices are set against altogether more powerful institutions—ranging from the contemporary media to sponsored think tanks and associated 'experts' brewing up political 'common sense'—in a conjuncture marked by continuing colonial warfare (Palestine, Iraq, Afghanistan, Libya, Syria, Mali, etc.) that seeks to endorse the global triumph of neoliberalism as a public discourse.

We, too, are learning, nothing is guaranteed. Rights and freedoms can be rolled back. If the Egyptian revolutionary charge can spiral down into military dictatorship, we in the West, held hostage to the logic of security, not to speak of the implacable economic 'laws of the market', can also experience a harsh downturn imposed by the unaccountable imperatives of governance. In a world that increasingly does not recognise human beings, only citizens and subjects, the categories that supposedly secure the polis are always open to unsuspected interpretation, redefinition, contestation, and ideological spin. Here our conceptual certainties become the agonistic sites of historical processes and cultural struggle that do not necessarily mirror only our critical and political imperatives. What has recently occurred in North Africa and the eastern Mediterranean throws an interrogating light across the West and its presumed separation from affairs elsewhere. Not only does a colonial past, etched in the actual frontiers of these states and, in particular, in the foundation of the state of Israel in 1948, continue to haunt the dramatic violence of the area, but understandings continue to be overwhelmingly directed and disciplined by Western figurations of Islam and the Arab world. In an under-read book by Edward Said—*Covering Islam: How the Media and the Experts Determine How We See the Rest of the World* (1981)—the precise political and cultural prison house of such constructions is caught in all of its brutal historical weight. Precisely by slipping beyond, reworking and transforming them, the West is now confronted by a modernity that is not merely 'ours' to administer and define. In the transit of translation, that as Walter Benjamin has taught us is always a two-way process in which the original is subsequently impossible to preserve from contamination, unexpected versions emerge.

After all, explanations that run along the grooves of precarious livelihood, youth unemployment, and the frequent unaccountability of government are an increasingly global condition and not simply restricted to the souths of the planet. Revolts in Tunis and rioting in south London are not the same thing. They are differentiated in all manner of complexities, but they are also bound together in the overarching procedures of a neoliberal global order. All of this is further amplified by the arrival of migrants in southern Europe, many of whom rightly insist that they are refugees fleeing 'our' wars and the decomposition of a European inheritance in Syria, Afghanistan, and the Horn of Africa. Here, in the resonance and dissonance of different localities we touch the paradoxes of the present conjuncture: registering in the Arab world demands for a better life that require change and accountable government, while in the West these perspectives are often publicly in retreat. To register the proximity of the dramatic presence of events unfolding on the African and Asian shores of the Mediterranean draws the West, however reluctantly, out of its self. Massacres, dictatorships, police brutality, people on the street seemingly responding to the sacred lexicon of Western liberalism—freedom, democracy—cannot be ignored. There was no burning of U.S. or European or Israeli flags; simply the disquieting spectacle of people apparently taking the political rhetoric of the West seriously; often far more seriously than the West itself. The languages of the Occident have now exceeded any single point of 'origin'; they are clearly no longer its property, to be defined and managed solely according to its exclusive needs.

What is exposed, in what until yesterday were the autocratic states of North Africa, is a profound challenge to neoliberalism, to its individualist and fundamentally anti-social and anti-democratic logic.[19] What has emerged in the Arab world is the fundamental contestation of the hypocrisy of the modern state, particularly after the fiscal crash of 2007, which considers the welfare of only its elites throughout the world. The majority of the population is cut out of the equation, reduced to the formula of policing dissent and profiling resistance. There is a significant planetary communality here. The public financing of stability and not of change, the rescue of banks and the bailing out of corruption rather than people, is part of a planetary drive towards privatising profits and socialising losses. Ultimately, the ongoing struggles for change in the Arab world is profoundly about processes of democratisation; not only about their failures and their absence in the rest of the world, *but also in the West itself.* All of this suggest that we consider an: 'Egypt that is not stuck in the past, clamouring for a future that Western democratic states have already attained. Rather, with a deeply entrenched and normalised state of emergency and its decades-old "war on terror", the kind of state that Egypt has become represents one potential secular future towards which Western democratic states are moving.'[20]

Abu Atris, the pseudonym of a writer working in Egypt, suggested on the Al Jazeera English website on February 24, 2011, that what was under way in the revolts in North Africa was a revolt against neoliberalism and the governance of its logic by subordinate client states in the Arab world. The systematic conflation of business and politics, forcibly bringing society under the rule of the market, is not only typical of the situation in 'advanced Western democracies'. Egypt and Tunisia have been neoliberal states for decades. The proximity of Arab leadership to Occidental administrations has been mirrored in public figures (which in Egypt includes the military leadership) having a foot in both politics and business. Government is there to defend free market fundamentalism, to divert financing from the public to the private sector, or rather to privatise and plunder public resources, and to ideologically block considerations of poverty and questions of social and economic justice. This is all part of the emerging state of perpetual war on the poor of the world: those without property and therefore according to classic liberal ideology, ultimately without rights.[21]

All of this also involves appreciating how our existing frameworks of political and cultural understanding can come unstuck as they are stretched (as Fanon would have put it) in their engagement with the novelty and the unexpected that revolt and revolution releases. The singularity of such events and their refusal to respect the premises of Occidental provenance (while the Western model is always present in the counter-revolutions that reimpose political stability for economic extraction) sustains the urgency for new modes of critical thought that are uncoupled from the triumphant narratives that confirm the authority of the Occident.[22] Here definitions and time scales fall apart as they refuse to accept an imposed chronology. Who decides when the revolution is over? Or whether one occurred? Are these definitions to be left only to Western observers and experts who, while often reluctant to grant the status of revolution to events in 2011 were immediately ready to adopt the terminology of counter-revolution in the explanation of subsequent developments. So, something did happen. As we have noted in the case of Iran, such questions, and the legitimation of their semantics, can produce twists and turns in a series of historical rhythms that will always escape our orchestration.

BEYOND THE BOUNDARY

C.L.R. James, author of *The Black Jacobins* (1938) also wrote a famous book on cricket: *Beyond a Boundary* (1963).[23] The Trinidad intellectual narrates how cricket, a sport developed on the playing fields of England, became a site in the West Indies for the 'clash of race, caste and class'.[24] In colonial spaces, the rules and practices of the game were reassembled as instances of resistance and renewal. This suggestive idea can also be extended to other areas of the colonial inheritance that include the philosophical lexicon and the political practices of the West. To run with this idea would be to acknowledge the inevitable break down in unilateral understandings. There exists no level playing field where all the participants are equal. This renders initial premises susceptible to new interpretations. For the problem, and moving from the cricket field to the intricate play of planetary powers, is that there does not exist a unique or homogeneous West, or East; there exists no such *thing* as Islam or Christianity. The world cannot be divided and separated out in such simplicities, and civilisation or truth cannot be immediately identified with one or other of the antagonistic poles. From this awareness it becomes possible to grasp the sense of an eventual humanism that is disentangled from the hypocrisy of a 'Europe which never stops talking of man yet massacres him at every one of its street corners, at every corner of the world'.[25] The humanism that Fanon here sought, to replace all those 'Mediterranean values, the triumph of the individual, of enlightenment and Beauty' that turn into 'pale, lifeless trinkets' and 'a jumble of dead words' has the vital responsibility to host requests and desires that exceed the will of the West.[26] To cross this threshold is to sound the intellectual and moral bankruptcy of Europe. It is to expose in the colonial apparatus the institutional racism that was the founding structure of Occidental modernity. Here it becomes increasingly significant to register the vicinity of Fanon and Foucault around the central idea of race and racism as a key discursive regime in the disposition of modern bio-politics.[27]

Together with its associated secularism, the public sphere is considered central to the formation and exercise of modern democracy. Here in the shared exposition of individualism and rationalised interests the modern bourgeois order was apparently formed.[28] It tends to be assumed that the rest of the world lives the concept of the public sphere as an absence, rather than historically proposing other modalities of public encounter, confrontation, and expression.[29] The opacity of embedded practices and lives elsewhere frequently confounds Occidental rationality seeking to render the world accountable to its sense of the self. If modern anthropology has begun to understand this, much of the rest of the social and human sciences still remain very much in the dark. What emerges is that the Occidental blueprint cannot be simply copied or imposed. Its languages and technologies may well open up local counter-spaces and narratives—from rap music, heavy metal Islam, and social networks to acquiring public presence and pressuring political institutions into radical change—but they are always in transit, without guarantees; their apparent roots in the West can also become somebody else's routes. The West in becoming the world loses its 'origins'.

The question of secularism and the public sphere should therefore not be understood simply in terms of a singular sociological specificity: the product of local forces and political practices. As part of historical processes they contribute to an altogether more extensive debate, and the eventual elaboration of a convivial critical space that is neither limited to Islam, the Arab world, nor to the West. The translation by the West of its external and subordinated other, and that of the West by the other, however asymmetrical the relationship, is by no means a one-way traffic. This is why the planetary transit of the West—its political languages, technologies, and modalities of knowledge—poses a far more significant perspective than that of merely instrumental mimicry, mistranslation and presumed 'betrayals'. In this sense the daily practices of realising political processes able to negotiate and configure the historical and cultural conditions of life in North Africa and the eastern Mediterranean pose a series of interrogations that simultaneously arrive at the heart of the global pretensions of democratic thought. The assumption that democracy is forever Occidental in provenance, practice, and participation necessarily comes undone. If the West has become the world it can no longer claim to be modernity's unique authority.

As the diasporic passages of music can teach us, the discourse and structures of democracy, religious faith and the public sphere can be duplicated, dubbed, and remixed in multiple versions. The encounter with other historical traditions, cultural patrimonies and modalities of reasoning instigates *mutual translation* (however uneven the forces in play). Freedom and democracy are not exportable items, religion is not merely a timeless dogma: all are historical practices that emerge from complex cultural fashioning. Learning from a multifarious world that has not simply been separated in its thought and culture from the West, but is also directly and deeply imbricated in its formation and language (from science and medicine to language, literature, and the culinary arts), is not merely a matter of adjusting a repressed historical archive.

Listening and responding to the southern and eastern shores of the present-day Mediterranean is, despite its obvious economic and political subordination to Euro-American interests, to take an apprenticeship in the justice of a democracy yet to come: both there and here. Such a perspective clearly impinges on a radical revaluation of the making and conceptualisation of modern urban space, of the bio-political logics and languages that seek to maintain and promote confines and borders, of the associated political and cultural geographies of belonging. Today this troubled First World inheritance feels it is under siege and invariably responds with a paranoid politics and a parochial policing of its confines.[30] This suggests the need to consider other ways of looking and reshaping the existing contours of sense. What is politically, culturally, and historically in play right now in the Mediterranean, particularly along its southern and eastern shores, is by no means merely of local significance. After being a consistently marginalised space in recent centuries, the Mediterranean has today rapidly become a laboratory of modernities in the making.

This, finally, is the 'disjunctive time'—to use Homi Bhabha's term—of the postcolonial present. It is a time that is neither linear nor monolithic, and exposes modernity to other dynamics.[31] It is right now being explored in events, cultural practices, and political struggles from Tunis to Teheran. This is a time that is divided from a unique temporality and is always out of joint with respect to a singular will. As a temporality that is folded into the uneven specificities of place, and their particular powers of transformation, it promotes the emerging critique of the assumed 'neutrality' of the Occidental view: its political framing, its historical verdicts, and the knowledge apparatuses of its social sciences. Political, sociological, and historical knowledge—their 'objectivity'—is rendered vulnerable, accountable in another, unsuspected critical space: all to be renegotiated in a displaced location where the Occidental subject is also destined to become the object of analysis.

COLONIALISM, CITIZENSHIP, RACE, AND DEMOCRACY

The accelerated hybridisation of Western society since the mid-twentieth century has accentuated the continuing reformulation of such key concepts as identity, nation, citizenship, society, democracy, and belonging. The existing political and historical script is unravelled to accommodate other possible narrations of a worldly modernity; a modernity that is not necessarily only 'ours' to manage and define. In this scenario, the stranger, as an unsettled and unsettling presence, the embodiment of a migrating modernity, becomes the political figure of our times. As Paul Gilroy has effectively put it: 'The automatic assumption that European history will be told best and most powerfully when it is made to coincide with the fixed borders of its national states will also have to be disposed of'.[32]

As we have already noted, concentrated in the stranger, today embodied, above all, in the contemporary migrant, is the profound interrogation and subsequent interruption of a precise cultural and historical formation that now finds its practices and definitions disturbed. We are confronted with limits: the limits of inherited definitions and the disciplinary procedures that reproduce and legitimate their logics. Such a discussion takes place in a situation in which political rights (even in their most bland liberal version) are today being rolled back to expose democratic states without democracy. The assumed inevitability of development and progress, in both economic and political terms, is now tottering on the edge of crisis and potential breakdown. The positivity of a linear, 'progressive' time slips sidewards into seemingly unknown scenarios. Meanwhile, agglomerations of unaccountable political and economic power are girding themselves to meet a multiplication of challenges and threats. The future, our future, is being colonised and disciplined for all eventualities, the doors on diversity are being bolted by discrimination. Concepts of citizenship and rights are under siege, legal definitions are sharpening the knives of distinction. A political space is being transformed into a policed one, typified by what Étienne Balibar would call 'conflictual citizenship'.[33] There is an emerging struggle over terms and prospects: who, what, where and how does an individual become a citizen?

Not only is citizenship being exposed to definition and redefinition, but also its presumed guarantee by institutional democracy is itself undergoing frequently unobserved revision and restriction. The global claims of Enlightenment ideas—often betrayed in practice from their very beginnings—have run up against a wall. They are now hung out to dry on the wires of security, patrolled by the fear that the world out there is running loose and no longer respecting its protocols. The processes apparently released by the West on the world in the name of modernity have seemingly turned against its control of the narrative.

Despite the liberal rhetoric of universalism that has philosophically accompanied its development, the political economy that came to dominate the world from the seventeenth century onwards is the product of a precise time and place. Between locality and universalism there lies an acute tension; a tension that is enacted in philosophical, political, racial, ecological and cultural terms. If Adam Smith proposed the unlimited laying up of the wealth of nations, thereby announcing the criteria for modern capitalist accumulation, the burgeoning economy of liberalism was also wedded to the idea of limitless moral and political resources. The twentieth century has consistently provided a series of brutal lessons that undo such illusions: from structural racism and genocide to ecological breakdown and economic collapse. The languages and institutions of knowledge are also deeply imbricated in this manner of narrating the world, as they continue to propose rationalised perspectives and confident solutions.

As we have already noted, the risk today is that social and cultural analysis, advanced in accredited journals, research exercises and academic evaluations, is increasingly over-determined by scholarly protocols and social science paradigms that are themselves part of the reproductive mechanism that the analysis ought critically to be seeking to contest. This economy of knowledge, like the limitless accumulation presumed to lie in the material and ecological resources of the planet, believes that it can expand continually in order to renew and reproduce itself and finally get the picture right; that there are limits, boundaries, incomprehensions, possible breakdowns and barriers, is rarely considered. Yet the overlooked matters of racism, the excluded histories of those rendered subaltern in ethnic, gendered and sexual marginalisation, the negated cultures of a rejected world, cannot simply be incorporated in the next theoretical wave. We need today to puncture and forcefully interrogate this consensual economy. There arrives a moment that involves undoing the powers and knowledge that mapped the preceding order before another configuration can emerge.

So, we are assailed by a persistent interrogation: is it the case that we adjust or more radically adjudicate the system in which we are caught? We are suspended between pragmatic choices elaborated in a fading, and failed, liberalism and the desire for something else, something more that draws us into an alternative critical space with respect to established procedures and protocols. A set of interrogations is set in motion that cracks the screen of 'scientific' neutrality and annuls the measured distance of the social scientist from his or her object of inquiry.[34] Beyond the patronising platitudes of present-day multiculturalism, the critical evaluation of the racist formation and the exercise of Occidental bio-power take us well beyond ideas of social adjustment, historical recognition and cultural 'toleration'. There is something altogether more extensive and profound involved here. Whether we like it or not, a conceptual and historical rigour propels us into a radical revaluation of our past, present and future. In its becoming central, and not peripheral, to the historical formation and cultural constellation of Occidental modernity, the power of the question of race promotes an unredeemable breach in the neutral whiteness of the social sciences paradigm.

For the remainders and reminders of race draw us into the processes and structures of power and exploitation that orbit along the implacable path of planetary capitalism: 'You are rich because you are white, you are white because you are rich'.[35] The dove-tailing of the declared 'objectivity' of the social sciences in the First World with the bio-political economy of modernity is clearly unable to reply to the demands its 'objects' pose when they insist on their rights to be historical subjects and narrate their versions of modernity. From the southern shore of the Mediterranean, from the south of the world, what does history, sociology or political science have to say to these words of Assia Djebar: 'Don't claim to "speak for" or, worse, to "speak on", barely speaking next to, and if possible *very close to*'.[36] This is what the anthropologist Paul Rabinow once suggestively called a 'mode of adjacency'.[37]

Here, as Jacques Derrida says, the embedded, lived-in, site of the city, rather than the abstract space of the nation, provides the laboratory for this more immediate and constantly negotiated becoming of belonging and democracy.[38] The barriers and blocking mechanisms of abstract state legislation often come to be blunted and diverted in the textures and issues of everyday urban existence. If the procedures of power are exercised by the law, the realities of street life, cultural proximities and neighbouring histories often lead to tactical gaps, negotiations and compromise. It is precisely here that the capitalist organisation and disarticulation of the 'social' is most effectively challenged. It is here that the structural logic of capital, seeking to colonise not simply the present but also the future, is most sharply exposed in its quotidian details and dangers. It is also here that oppositional and alternative counter-narratives and subterranean histories of modernity acquire substance, a life, and flesh.

Everyday racism, encountered on the streets, in the bus queues, the shops and the neighbourhood, cuts into the political and cultural fabric of modern life. Taking account of its violence and divisive logics, tracking its multiple expressions, its media amplifications, and mapping an affective cultural economy of fear and hatred are some of the tasks required in countering it. That immediate goal, however, cannot be a political solution. Perhaps racism is itself a direct offspring of the precise construction of existing political formations and what we call the 'public sphere'. For these are spaces that are never simply open. They have consistently been constituted through inclusions and exclusions, through possibilities of access, control, and negation; and, above all, through the shifting political, cultural, and historical orchestration of what passes for 'identity' and 'belonging' (national, civic, cultural, historical, gendered, ethnic). At one time, for example, in the United States, Irish, and Italians were not considered 'white'; women were until recently excluded from the political and public sphere in all Western democracies. This is perhaps why, ultimately, illiberalism is constitutive of liberalism. It is here that a crucial distinction begins to open up between ideas of future democracy and the existing practices of multiculturalism. Recognising and registering cultural difference does not automatically produce more democracy; it can even lead to a retrenchment of rights throughout the public sphere as each constituency forcefully insists on its own particular claims. As Seyla Benhabib has argued, it is rather through embracing creolising processes and hybridising practices that a more dynamic democracy becomes possible.[39]

To pose the question of illiberal practices in contemporary Europe is very much about taking democracy and its liberal rhetoric seriously: pushing it to the edge, exposing its limits. It is also about taking its historical and cultural formation seriously. This means to confront in its structural authority the exercise of sanctioned violence that is not simply physically repressive, but, above all, linguistically and legally so. These days this is most sharply in evidence around questions of immigration and the subsequent negation of human and civil rights. As Alessandro Dal Lago tellingly puts it: the state today does not recognise human rights, only the rights of its citizens.[40] By way of Homeland Security, the UK Border Agency, Fortex, and the generalised criminalisation of immigration in the First World, the modern state now explicitly rejects Article 13 of the 1948 United Nations Declaration on Human Rights that endorsed the right of movement in and between states. It is at this point that we concur with the Moroccan sociologist Mehdi Alioua that we need to rethink migration as a project of freedom.[41] How is it possible to reattain a 'freedom' that was unilaterally exercised for many centuries by the West in its appropriation of the planet?

The contemporary denial of the right to movement and migration produces the dramatic theatre of modern political and geographical power: between South and North; Africa, Asia, and Latin America to one side, Europe, Australia, and North America to the other. This is increasingly accompanied by the erection of real, physical walls. Digging deeper into the argument we are forced to acknowledge that the present response of government to extra-

European immigration is not merely a political reply to immediate xenophobia fuelled by economic and social crises. Beyond repressive legislation there is a structural violence inherited in particular modalities of reason that have historically emerged in the persistent gap between European humanism, its moral philosophy, and the practices of the West both at home and abroad.

To think of the crucial interrelationship between colonialism, citizenship, and democracy in the elaboration of Occidental modernity is to acknowledge a historical violence both in the colonial cut and the subsequent postcolonial wound that bleeds into all accountings of the past and the present. It is to register ideas of race and practices of racism being constitutive of modern Occidental citizenship. It not a residual element but rather a regulatory mechanism that dramatically collates yesterday's slave trade with present-day immigration policies and police profiling.[42] This disturbing and unruly inheritance is further augmented now that the controlling distance of a colonial 'abroad' is no longer available: Algeria, the Caribbean, Somalia, India, all are 'here' amongst us. Such proximities are the often unwelcome social (and political) side of globalisation. It is precisely such intimacies, encountered in the cities, streets and cultures of the so-called First World, that dramatically accentuate the planetary scale of the cruel interval between social and historical justice and the brutal immediacy of the law.[43]

To reference present-day racisms is to register the reductive reach of the polity. The latter continually oversteps the seemingly liberal agenda of community and the bland superficialities of 'multiculturalism' to impose the law on those bodies considered external to its institutions. Such bodies are invariably understood as a 'problem': potential disturbers and saboteurs of its authority. Unregistered, hence 'illegal', immigrants employed in 'dirty work' by capital in the grey areas of the economy are perpetually exposed to the arbitrary violence of the law. If they remain inert they are invisible, if they seek to move they are destined to be documented in the machinery of the judiciary. In both cases, they are subjected to aggressive popular sentiment cultivated in the ready explanations provided by the mass media. There is barely a whiff of interest in the immigrant as a human, social, and historical being. What counts is the power—social, cultural, historical, political and, above all, economic—exercised over him or her as an object of economic, legal, cultural, and political identification. Through such practices, so-called foreign bodies are estranged and externalised, rendered both anonymous and silent by the very laws and procedures that the liberal state elaborates to sustain its legitimacy. Whatever else you are, you have already been identified as being 'out of place' and fixed as an immigrant, a Muslim, a black, a potential subverter of the existing order.

To challenge contemporary racism, then, is ultimately to challenge a political and cultural formation that continues to benefit from its existence and exercise. This is to consider what Eyal Weizman has called 'lawfare'. This is constituted by mobile nets of legality that can be extended and withdrawn by a punitive political: from the open-air prison of the Gaza Strip to patrolling the Mediterranean and transforming migration into an illegal condition.[44] In other words, injustice is sustained in a net of legal technologies; the law sustains injustice. Power is legally sanctioned, and institutional racism is held up in the courts. In the end, as recent decades have clearly taught us, all injustices and atrocities can be legally justified. To step beyond the law, in order to reaffirm law and authority, has accustomed us to accept the creeping insistence of the exceptional state in a mesh of legislation and dispositions, quotidian techniques and routines, institutional practices and know-how, and their increasing application and perfection. This is the 'banality of evil'— exposed in Walter Benjamin's noted essay on the legalisation of violence, in Hannah Arendt's verdict on Eichmann, and recently recalled in Judith Butler's significant critique of Zionism—that the state perpetuates in binding citizens to its rule.[45] Proudly announced on British trains transporting passengers to and fro between Gatwick and Heathrow airports, the UK Border Agency lists its successes, aided by the latest technologies and the booming industry of surveillance, in tracking down illegal immigration and keeping 'our' borders safe. These borders are certainly not safe for human beings, in fact they are increasingly dangerous and life-threatening; they are only relatively secure for those who can claim a locatable citizenship and associated passport.

The modern establishment of the rule of law was accompanied by the simultaneous production of the ghetto, plantation slavery (probably the largest industrial enterprise in the world in the seventeenth and eighteenth centuries), indentured labour, the concentration camp, and contemporary identification and transfer centres for illegal immigrants. All of these practices and associated technologies exist outside the time and space of the nation. They are located in that no-man's land that sustains the legal separation and political policing of catalogued bodies according to hierarchies of cultural worth beneficial to existing relations of power.[46] This is why, although the comparison is invariably avoided, the distance between the institutions of racist slavery of the eighteenth century that shadowed the birth of modern Atlantic economies and their political democracies, and today's so-called illegal immigration, is far closer than the intervening two centuries might suggest. It is precisely this black hole at the centre of Occidental life that is most sharply underlined by Sibylle Fischer when she rightly argues, against Jürgen Habermas, that modernity is not an unfinished or incomplete project but rather, and echoing Walter Benjamin, the site of an ongoing, complex and contested constellation of powers in which the violence and barbarism that is intrinsic to its founding and practice is rarely understood or registered:

the modernity that took shape in the Western Hemisphere (in theoretical discourse as well as in cultural and social institutions) in the course of the nineteenth century contains, as a crucial element, the suppression of a struggle whose aim was to give racial equality and racial liberation the same weight as those political goals that came to dominate nineteenth century politics and thought—most particularly, those relating to nation and national sovereignty. Unless we submit the concept of modernity to a radical critique, our emancipatory goals and strategies will continue to reproduce the biases that came to shape modern thought in the Age of Revolution.[47]

To contest the racist practices of disciplinary powers that articulate the cultural protocols of a historical formation—the human and social sciences of Occidental modernity—we paradoxically turn to the very laws whose historical formation legitimates their authority and the present-day sovereignty of the modern state. Confronted with the declared neutrality of the social sciences (notwithstanding their lengthy historical involvement in racial definitions and racist judgements), we explore their languages precisely in order to excavate the continual shortfall of an ethical and democratic sense of the political. This clearly does not simply involve contesting the existing neoliberal state and its delegation of economic and, above all, social, powers, and decisions to the abstract laws of the 'market'. It is also, and most precisely, about radically reconsidering the historical and cultural formations that have created this state of affairs. Michel Foucault once suggested that we should be looking for a new set of rights that are both anti-disciplinary and 'emancipated from the principle of sovereignty'.[48]

The prevalent bio-politics that has identified in racial typologies and national identities a sovereign power to be exercised in the public pursuit of its legitimacy is, as Foucault pointed out, a juridical edifice of legal rights that exercises command and subjugation.[49] In other words, the very definitions of race, cultural identity, and historical belonging are not simply contested fields where common sense has to be challenged. They are also, and most pointedly, critical nodes around which a very different understanding of political configurations needs to be constructed. What precisely does existing politics and its associated *doxa* seek to obscure and disqualify? To answer this question is not merely to register the repression that accompanies hegemonic representations, it is also to engage with the stuff and textures of quotidian experience; it is to move in the folds of an affective cultural economy in which histories and cultures are inscribed, inflected and deflected: all is susceptible to the transit and transformation that accompanies translation; that is, interpretation.

This, however, need not be the only manner in which to acknowledge a differentiated and planetary modernity. In claiming a modernity that is otherwise, we need to identify that 'insurrection of subjugated knowledges' that promote a diverse archaeology of the present.[50] The latter produces a very different archive and, with it, a very different sense of the historical composition and genealogy of modernity with which to invest contemporary understandings. Here the archive proposes not an act of conservation but one of redistribution, not so much a custody of the past as a claim on the future. Such a disturbance in the routinised field of vision scratches the lens of Occidental hegemony. Epidermal distinctions and associated hierarchies are set adrift, crossed, and contested by sounds, signs and silences off-screen, outside the frame. Within the proximity of such counter-histories the assumed continuity of sovereignty breaks down into multiple tempos and experiences.[51]

The sense of such a constellation can no longer be considered in a unilateral manner, or as the mere accumulation of 'progress', or the simple reflection of a 'universal' form: capital, modernity, the West. In this insurrectionary perspective, race is never given. It names a dynamic, an array of possibilities and powers, in which the unacknowledged enigma is whiteness, its biopolitical hegemony and assumed supremacy. The colonisation of bodies by colour (Fanon) is a historical process, rather than an ontological constant; it operates with shifting confines and temporalities. It acquires an intensity in certain situations and conditions, and becomes a differentiating, political device. It draws on something that matters; this is matter—skin pigmentation, cultural difference, historical distinctions—that establishes something else: political power, cultural hegemony. It is a dynamic assemblage, rather than a simple state of identity.[52] For race is not simply about bodies and prejudices, it is also inscribed in the distribution of social and urban space; it produces the form and content of the modern city; it sustains the present ranking of political and cultural power. . . . Race is an arrangement of powers.[53] It is the articulation of 'race' through identified bodies, epidermal traits, religion, class, and cultural markers that produces the overdetermined interpretive grid of the Muslim and the 'mugger', the 'terrone', and the 'terrorist'.[54]

This is not a neutral verdict. In other words, race as a discursive force, inscribed in a material set of practices and institutions, is produced by a particular aggregation of power, and is deployed to ensure its reproduction. Race is itself the materialisation of the hierarchies of power that produce it as a category. The history of racism in the formation of Occidental modernity over the last five centuries is precisely the largely unacknowledged, but highly visible, articulation of that mechanism: that 'heart of darkness' embodied in the education and legislation of its social bodies. Race, and the violent geographies of the world that produced modernity, is still very much an active script. Without race, and the accompanying repertoire of racisms, white hegemony, no longer able to project itself through subordinate others, would falter. Its mechanisms of power, now historically specified, culturally located and deprived of universal legitimacy, would collapse in on itself. The increasingly vicious turn in present-day racism, accompanied by a mounting xenophobia, is perhaps the displaced recognition of this emerging scenario. Being white now becomes an anxious, even 'nervous' condition (Frantz Fanon).

This encourages us into considering what is the economic, cultural, and social work achieved by race in producing an affective political landscape. It most obviously activates a classificatory logic for identifying disturbance and the refusal of an existing state of affairs when underpaid illegal migrant workers refuse their inhuman conditions of employment, or when there is no longer a unique religious custom that commands: minarets in the heart of Christendom. Here, where the colonial world of yesterday is rendered immediate in the modern metropolis we are drawn into the planetary coordinates of exploitation as they are redrawn in the heteronomy of increasingly shared spaces. And here, returning to those minarets, questions of cultural difference increasingly become part of the construction of social, historical, cultural and political matters. Here 'private' religious concerns constitute public and symbolic spaces whose racial inscription and ethnic construction inevitably support racist agendas, including those of the presumed Christian formation of 'secular' Europe.[55]

As a language, a concept, a practice, and a contingent event, racism cannot be resolved. It is part of a far wider state of affairs whose powers and authority constitute the very horizon of contemporary political, cultural, and economic power and their associated sense. This particular world is not about to relinquish its powers; it is, on the contrary, further buttressing them in increasingly contorted legal strictures and structures. Racism is central to the present making of the modern world. It is part and parcel of the promotion of hegemony. Here racism takes us beyond race into the altogether more vulnerable understanding of a modernity that is neither made nor warranted by any singular history or culture. This is to wrench the question of race away from the limited parameters of immediate political agendas. For the question of race and racism draw us ever deeper into the recognition and contestation of the structural inequalities that produce the planetary ubiquity of social violence and historical injustice.

NOTES

1. Chakrabarty 2007.
2. Baldwin 1972, 87–88.
3. Khaldûn 2005, 5.
4. Hauser 1999.
5. Habermas 1992.
6. The ten African and European cities evoked here refer to a project called Ten Cities, promoted by the Goethe Institute in Nairobi. The project considers the construction and extension of public space through music, DJ practices, dance and critical discussion. Details are

available at http://blog.goethe.de/ten-cities. It can also be consulted in series of essays published in Hossfeld 2017.
7. Eley 2002, 224.
8. Featherstone 2008.
9. Elizabeth Freeman quoted in Stacey 2016.
10. Chalcraft 2016, 3–4.
11. Tazzioli 2015, ix.
12. Chalcraft 2016. On the deployment of E.P. Thompson's concept of the 'moral economy of the crowd' in the historical investigation of modern Islam and social movements, see Burke 1988.
13. De Smet 2016.
14. Parvan 2014.
15. Foucault, "A Powder Keg Called Islam", quoted in Afary and Anderson 2004.
16. Hallaq 2013, 14.
17. Fahmy 2015.
18. Alessandrini 2014.
19. For a succinct account in the case of Egypt, see Magdy 2014.
20. Hussein 2012.
21. Roy 2014.
22. For a further discussion on this point in the context of Foucault, Fanon, and the recent revolutions in North Africa, see Alessandrini 2014.
23. James 1989.
24. James 1994, 66.
25. Fanon 2004, 235.
26. Fanon 2004, 11.
27. Foucault 2004.
28. Habermas 1992.
29. Salvatore 2011.
30. Mohanty 2003.
31. Mezzadra and Rahola 2006.
32. Gilroy 2004, 164.
33. Balibar 2008.
34. Amin 2012.
35. Fanon 2004, 5.
36. Djebar 1992, 2.
37. Rabinow 2007, 49.
38. Derrida 2000.
39. Benhabib 2002.
40. Dal Lago 2009.
41. Alioua 2005, 185.
42. Mellino 2013.
43. Mbembe 2009.
44. Weizman 2009.
45. Benjamin 1999; Butler 2012.
46. Agamben 1998, 181.
47. Fischer 2004, 273 – 234.
48. Foucault 2004, 40.
49. Foucault 2004, 25.
50. Foucault 2004, 7.
51. Foucault 2004, 70.
52. Saldanha 2007.
53. Swanton 2008.
54. 'Terrone': of the earth, peasant, uncouth—the term of abuse that Northern Italians bestow on those coming from the Italian south. For the classic exposure of these mechanisms and practices, see Hall, Critcher, Jefferson, Clarke, and Roberts 2013.
55. Chambers 2013.

Chapter Five

Scarred Landscapes

In January 1948 a plane crash occurs in California, just south of San Francisco in the hills of Los Gatos. Angered by the manner in which the *New York Times* reported the death of the thirty-two people on the plane—naming the pilot, co-pilot, stewardess and the immigration official, while referring to the twenty-eight illegal workers being returned to Mexico simply as deportees—the American songwriter Woody Guthrie wrote the lyrics for what would become the song 'Plane Wreck at Los Gatos (Deportee)'. It is probably most noted in one of the many versions by Joan Baez, but we can also listen to a more avant-garde bluesy version recorded in June 2011 in Palermo, Sicily, by the English musician Mike Cooper.[1]

Picking strawberries, lettuce, and fruit in southern California, picking tomatoes and oranges in southern Italy: cheap, underpaid, and illegal labour, close to slavery. This is a story of illegal migration, oppression, and misery that runs from southern California to southern Italy (from Los Gatos to the island of Lampedusa just off the North African coast, to the towns of Rosarno in Calabria and Castel Volturno in Campania). It also propels us back in time, spiralling down into the depths of Paul Gilroy's Black Atlantic and the slave ships criss-crossing the Atlantic between Africa and the Americas while laying the foundations of today's global political economy. Then forward into the present again and the small boats crossing today's Mediterranean, poetically and politically figured in Isaac Julien's three screen video installation *Western Union. Small Boats* (2007). Seemingly different times and locations come together in shared historical testimony within a common critical constellation.

So, why the song? First, because it refers us to the historical continuity of migration, drawing our attention to its structural centrality in the making of the modern world. At the same time, the song also invites us to consider the means of memory. From the psychoanalytical writing pad to the cinema and music, memory requires a means, a medium. Further, to consider the means of memory is to consider the nature of the archive and the manner of archiving. What is legitimated and what is excluded becomes explicit in the forms, technologies, and organisation of knowledge: this is the power and the authority of the archive and its institutional registration in school and university textbooks, museums, popular representations, and ultimately common sense. Thus the song, in both the materiality of sound and the largely unsung history of migration, proposes an archaeology of unsuspected, clandestine memories that promote another history. Conscious and unconscious recall—both that recognised, and that repressed and refused—solicit the question of the archive, a question here sustained in sound. This means to cross the claims of institutional history, the accumulated power of its narrative, with the disturbing traces of memories that scratch and finally cut into the corpus of its pretensions, producing an open and incurable wound. It is to recognise with Paul Ricœur that

> there exists no historical community that has not been born out of a relation that can, without hesitation, best be likened to war. What we celebrate under the title of founding events are, essentially, acts of violence legitimated after the fact by a precarious state of right.[2]

Like Mike Cooper's version of 'Plane Wreck at Los Gatos (Deportee)', this is a blues version of modernity, a dark counter-history, that insists on the dissent notes that stretch the official account until it tears, and in the break releases another story of our time.[3] This is ultimately to tap into the deeper currents of the black Atlantic diaspora—its poetics and politics—and into its centrality in the making of modernity.[4] Of course, this has found little space in the official narratives of national histories, their explanations of the modern world and their transformation of the past into the exhibition spaces of the museum, the art galley, and the school text book. Here there lies a critical, even explosive, link between the largely repressed historical memory of other migrations and the radical revaluation of modernity announced in the illicit passage, presence, and narratives of contemporary migrants. As we have seen, the juridical-political regime that today marks, catalogues and defines the migrant's body as an object of economic, legal, and political authority, consistently exposes the long-standing Occidental imperative to reduce the globe to its needs. It reopens the colonial archive and the political economy that initially established this planetary traffic in bodies, capital, goods. While whites who migrate today are apparently expats, the term 'migrant' is racially reserved for those who arrive from the so-called global south. The economic order does not simply reflect but rather justifies power. Once it is set to another rhythm, narrated according to another marking of time, another body of experience, sounded with subaltern inflections, accented by a different beat, *that* history turns out to be neither single nor without alternative tellings.

An acquired fluidity, an excess of time and a supplement of sense, encourages a remapping and reworking of inherited traditions and their transmission in a manner that precisely privileges the *transit* and *transformation* of history, memory, and belonging. This is the vulnerable space of cultural translation that is always under construction. After all, what is this memory but a site of images with its gaps, jumps, slow motion, and fast-forward? The historian's drive for seeming objectivity (according to whose paradigm, where and how?) surely misses the point of critical honesty. It is not a purported objective truth that draws us on. As Jacques Le Goff pointed out, 'the document is not objective raw material, but expresses past society's power over memory and over the future: the document is what remains'.[5] The prospect of history is a 'problematic'; what Le Goff himself calls the 'history of history'.[6] The coordinates of time, place and belonging, rendered critical, inevitably introduce us to their social production and historical fabrication. According to Le Goff the 'basic material of history is time'.[7] If this is so, it is a poly-rhythmic and multi-accented materiality that produces diverse spaces and places. It suggests discontinuous, sedimented, and multi-tiered temporalities: whose time, whose events impact on the construction and organisation of the calendar? I will return to this argument in more detail in the final chapter.

WHOSE ARCHIVE?

The phrase the 'landscape is the ultimate archive', pronounced not so long ago by the Lebanese artist Akram Zaatari, brings us to consider how we are placed.[8] The articulation of memory, the past, together with institutional recollections, always occurs somewhere, in a location. And if there is a place where memories and meanings are sedimented and laid up that is in the material insistence, persistence and transformation of the landscape. Of course, what is in the land is often illegible, if not covered up and invisible. It is an archive that houses the inscrutable, but nevertheless crucial, conditions of our existence. In the landscape there also exist altogether more obvious archives. These are social artefacts and constructions. They take the form of museums, galleries, exhibitions, textbooks, buildings: structures and practices that sustain the official inscriptions of time. These public archives are invariably driven by the desire to confirm the present. What is represented and exhibited between the walls and among the pages of the catalogue, the guidebook and the television program, stands in for a particular arrangement and order of sense. The latter is secured in protocols and premises that appeal to the presumed neutrality of scientific research, objectivity and 'balance'. The museum, for example, as an exercise in the rationalisation of time and space, seeks to render these coordinates natural and universal. Its configuration, just like that of the social and human sciences from where it draws its authority, is an invention of European modernity. Its strengths and shortcoming derive from these premises.

Insisting on such confines proposes the possibility of unexpected encounters with the past. This can lead to perforating those pretensions of the present that consider the past as though it were really over. For history, as Freud and psychoanalysis have taught us, is ultimately a narration of what has seemingly elapsed in the process of producing a future. In the complicities of remembering, history unconsciously speaks of a past—negated, displaced, mis-recognised—that is yet to be told. It promotes a ruin, a relic of the previous order of sense, and disrupts its physical and metaphysical premises. Such a dismantling of the historical formation and cultural constellation of the West impacts directly on the public institutions of memory. It is here that the concept of the postcolonial becomes most acute as Euro-American coordinates and their planetary pronouncements come to be interrogated. This is precisely why there is little point in modern museum and art curators confidently announcing in their global scrutiny that postcolonial arguments have little resonance in Asia or Latin America (where decolonial thinking is obdurately seeking to delink itself from Europe) and that therefore we can now terminate discussing it in Europe and North America. As though we can now simply step beyond that particular critical interrogation of Occidental authority and get back to working on the next theoretical turn with which to frame the world.

To continue to insist on the questions disseminated by postcolonial criticism and practices is to stretch and rework our understanding of the archive and leave it open to the uninvited guest and her unrecognised histories. Today, for many of the uninvited, their first taste of European hospitality and hostility is represented by the detention centre on the Italian island of Lampedusa. We are not simply on a rock covered by desert scrub some 200 kilometres south of the cities of Tunis and Algiers. We are in the south of Italy, of Europe, of the so-called First World, where geographical distance is annulled by political and cultural immediacies. Again we could consider this particular landscape, as Akram Zaatari suggests, as an archive. Composed of shipwrecked boats, fishermen, illegal migrants, state officials, tourists, shop and restaurant owners, this is a volatile contact zone where the south of the planet comes up, often violently, against, the over-developed world. Here we are drawn into considering how different memories of migration cross and compose the liquid archive of the Mediterranean: yesterday Europe's rural poor crossing its waters towards the Americas and North Africa; today, despite all the obstacles raised by Europe, those from Africa and Asia seeking refuge and a better life. Here the multiple souths of the planet crack and infiltrate the modernity that has consigned their histories to silence. Here the arbitrary violence of legality, rights, and citizenship are brutally exposed. If the present-day Mediterranean cemetery is witness to the necropolitics of global capital, it equally also registers the very limits of a European humanism and its historical order. Both pretend universal valence while continuing to subordinate the needs of the rest of the planet, or simply leaving them to sink beneath the waves, consigned to the abyss between the law and justice.

To consider the historical archive of this space—the Mediterranean—is also to trouble profoundly the prevalent historical placeholder of the modern nation state. This is to query what has come to be considered the *natural* form of historical formations; but history, as Hannah Arendt consistently argued, is clearly not only narrated, lived and perceived through the nation. This is to question both a political order of knowledge and its direct inscription in the disciplinary protocols of modern sociology, political science, area studies, anthropology, and historiography, not to speak of the assumed authority of national literatures and languages. Working in a Mediterranean web of trans-national histories, and their presence and effects on multiple scales, suggests even more: the conceptual landscape peculiar to one of its shores, in particular its northern, hegemonic European one, is now exposed to very different understandings and unsuspected variations. We are here drawn into a shifting geography of memory (and forgetting) where meaningful details are connected with forgotten futures: a dynamic interweaving of past and future collated in the intensities of the present.

Today the poor are not permitted to travel. They can only travel illegally, outside the confines imposed by First World law and the dictates of its version of the globe. Social injustice is directly inscribed in the legal frameworks established by a colonial inheritance and its contemporary disciplining of the planet. The contemporary migrant's story is precisely the exposure of this political economy. It cuts into all understandings of the modern world. It renders the procedures of explaining and exhibiting the past and the present altogether more opaque, complicated and necessarily incomplete. In the summer of 2013 a temporary exhibition entitled a 'Museum of Migration' was held in a space provided by the Lampedusa town council. Here mundane objects—a packet of couscous, a plastic sandal, a rusting tea pot—washed ashore or taken from abandoned boats, acquired a new density once they had been displaced from anonymous lives to the exhibition logic of the display case. What persists and resists in these objects is the violent interval that marks their passage from everyday life (and death) to this quayside building in the port of Lampedusa. They become the spectres of the neoliberal global order that in the end cannot be easily accommodated in the language of an exhibition. On the edge and beyond the frontiers of institutional legitimacy, the items housed in this temporary museum on this dusty island in the seas of

Tunisia refuse to lend themselves easily to the fetishisation of art. We are shifted from the finitude of the isolated object to the ongoing processes of a disquieting project and the situations it produces. In this particular locality, witnessing migrants receive a plastic bag that contains a panino, a two-litre bottle of water, a packet of ten cigarettes (only for the men), and a telephone card to phone home, before being shipped off to an identification centre in Sicily, the wound is too deep and too fresh. The colonial imperatives that seek to criminalise, racialise, and denigrate the other in their modern mobility are too close to the comfort of *our* lives.

How to narrate migration? Is it simply a social problem, an economic phenomenon, an individual drama always on the cusp of tragedy? Or is it an integral part of an extensive trans-national history driven by a planetary political economy that constantly reiterates the cruel archives of modernity in its practices of accumulation and exploitation? Today we live in the liberal fiction of 'intercultural dialogue', as though there is an ongoing exchange between different, but equal, partners in a multilateral world. This clearly negates the brutal evidence of the injustice of asymmetrical relationships of power. It ignores the uneven and unjust distribution of economic and cultural capital that has shaped the global formation of modernity. Some talk, some listen, and the majority are silent. Or, rather, that is the practice framed in Paris, New York, Rome, Berlin, Tel Aviv, or London. Of course, everyone, everywhere, is talking, but how much of that complex conversation gets to be registered, acknowledged and acquires authority, is altogether another story. Who, in the present political economy of the world, has the power to pronounce, to archive and exhibit?

It is at this point that the concept of the archive comes to be suggestively stretched to include other means and memories; for example, considering the sights and sounds of cinema, video, the visual arts and music that promote sites and situations where we continually respond to the present of the past. These languages sustain a perpetual exchange between deterritorialisation and reterritorialisation, between shifting configurations of past and present. They propose modernity as a site of perpetual transformation and unplanned translations. This leads to shifting the very premises of the archive and its mechanisms of collecting and cataloguing. Here, too, the classical instruments of sociology, anthropology, and art criticism frequently come unstuck. Robbed of a grounding in the relative stability of disciplinary and institutional referents, localised in a precise region of the planet and its chronologies, our very knowledge is subject to ethnographic inquiry.[9]

Here existing spatial and temporal coordinates are sundered to reveal other prospects, other archives. The critical gaze can no longer be secured in a single location. If the rhetoric of globalisation implicitly seeks to export and impose the unicity of a perspective of Occidental provenance, it is increasingly crossed and confuted by other views, or else, and more usually, ends up simply looking and talking to itself. Either way, the power of its critical valence is reduced. At this point, we are here no longer looking to the West, but through it towards further temporalities and spaces. Beyond the borderlands of indigenous museums where things are certainly on the move, this means to promote an ethnography not of the elsewhere, but of the West itself. It implies the explicit configuration of the why, what, where, when and how of collecting and exhibiting. It is no longer possible to remain within the security of a seemingly neutral exercise in the scientific taxonomies of knowledge. This draws us away from the precise European custody and imperial capture of an overarching 'universal' measure of the world towards the specificities of a planetary 'universality' that we have seen is ultimately irreducible to a single framing or explanation.[10]

Battlefields, war cemeteries, monuments, mausoleums, and museums are physically the most obvious symbolic sites of European society's 'difficult heritage'.[11] Elsewhere there also exists more insidious evidence traced in extra-European landscapes that have been riven and racialised by conflicts over the interpretation and representation of the past. To introduce race into the landscapes that sustain the archives of memory is to insist on the colonial fashioning of the modern world and the requisite decolonisation of space, temporality, and knowledge. Behind the European strife of the twentieth century, shaped and shattered by world wars and genocide, lie the longer and deeper histories of European colonialism and its imperialist apotheosis in the bio-political violence of the racist governance of the non-European world. This inheritance is inscribed in the very bodies and lives that were rendered subordinate objects in the procedures of European subjectivity, even when called upon to fight for Europe in anonymous colonial allegiance. Beyond the request to reconfigure the past to accommodate, respond and take responsibility for the structural occlusion and omission of the colonised world as an actor and maker of modernity lies the trauma of this truncated memory. These memories live on and are continually reactivated in the present. They are part of the texture of modern metropolitan life.

If in the depths of time there lies this archaeology of past matters, we also know that they remain, acknowledged or not, pertinent to the genealogy of the present. The contemporary is hence marked by an image of time that is always lacerated, creased, and incomplete. Memory is precisely the image of the presence of that absence. For memory, as the exercise of representation and repression, ultimately reveals the 'fundamental relation of history to violence'.[12]

Chapter 5
UNSUSPECTED GEOGRAPHIES

In this key, the review of the representation of the past is now located in a diverse heuristic space. Populating the present, refused bodies, memories and lives are profoundly interlocked in 'the problematic of the representation of the past'.[13] This, and setting Paul Ricœur in conversation with the French art critic and historian Georges Didi-Huberman, is to encounter the 'enigma of an image'. For images are always loaded with time; that is, with more time that any one of us can individually contain or comprehend.[14] The power of images is in their potential to explode the present and exceed the consensual manner of its framing. Proposing a history of art that exceeds linear affiliations in abstract chronologies is to disseminate holes in time.

The body of the native, the indigenous, the non-European, invariably non-white, but no longer a silent object, has today become a subjective and subjecting force that bends, folds and rewrites the imposed script of a prevalent historical and cultural intelligibility into another narrative, another telling of time and place. This leads to a new, unsuspected ecology of citizenship. Against the violence of the law that seeks to exclude such a possibility, 'my' history finds itself being traversed to accommodate other stories and voices. This is not merely about an aesthetic shift, or the emergence of a new genre, but is rather about historical appropriations that propose emergent forms of belonging. These may well be unauthorised, but they are socially real and destined to resist and persist. In such a constellation the critical operation perhaps lies less in perfecting a recovery of forgotten lives and unsung histories, and rather in radically reconfiguring existing history in order to install the intervals and interruptions that disturb its coherence and deviate the teleology that initially produced such silences and forgetting.

Consider John Akomfrah's strikingly poetical allegory on post-war immigration in Britain in the film *The Nine Muses* (2010). Black bodies in frozen landscapes cross and cut up the Western canon (both its sense of history and aesthetics): Caspar David Friedrich's *The Wanderer above the Mists* (1818), Coleridge's *The Rime of the Ancient Mariner* (1798), and Edgar Allan Poe's *The Narrative of Arthur Gordon Pym* (1838) offer hospitality to a black man in a yellow parka contemplating Arctic infinity. The repetition of accredited imagery and words (Samuel Beckett, T.S. Eliot, John Milton, etc.) underscores the mythical quality of the odyssey of migration from the Caribbean, Africa and the Indian sub-continent to the wasteland of post-war Britain while simultaneously taking us elsewhere, into another critical space. Akomfrah refuses to be simply 'black', and critically mixes a diasporic aesthetics into a new cultural mix. This history of migration eschews the empirical realism that would frame it in a precise socio-economic category or rigid temporality. It literally migrates, confusing and confuting the categories seeking to constrain and contain its cultural and historical challenge. Once again, beyond the boundary, this composite history unwinds across the whole panorama of modern Britain (and Europe). It can no longer be reduced to a limited identification in race, migration, or identity.

Routing such memories, practices, and proposals through unsuspected landscapes leads less to regaining an impossible past and rather in promoting an unsuspected access to the present that set different directions for the future. The institutional archive, its history, museums, and the ethnographic drive to objectify and define others is reworked and challenged—not so much from the past as from the becoming of the future that touches 'the legitimation of the duty of memory as a duty of justice'.[15] Such configurations uproot the authority of earlier perspectives and certainties. Considering history as a ruin we can draw critical energies freed from the illusion of a finished edifice. If this obviously references Walter Benjamin's famed angel of history staring backwards on the accumulated debris of the past while being blown ineluctably into the future, it also proposes the Deleuzian fold in time that shatters the superficial chronologies of historicism and accompanying sociological chatter.[16] A disruption and multiplication of historical rhythms finds in the ruin the accommodation of other tempos. In their improvised contingency they compose an accommodation that is still being worked on, that is never settled in definition.

Perhaps the recognition that historical and anthropological 'objects' housed in the Occidental archive have now refused such a status and insist on their rights to subjectivity and their narration of the world is similar in measure to the shattering European 'discovery' of both the New World and a heliocentric universe in the sixteenth century. Perhaps. In both cases, a cut is exercised on an existing body of knowledge and power. In both cases there lies the registration of a world whose excess interrogates and interrupts the stilled edification of the past articulated around the positive progress of the European self. Here we can turn back into the spirals of time accompanied by, for example, Frantz Fanon. For it has been, above all, Fanon who has taught us, as much as Foucault, about the objectification of bodies, histories and cultures, their classification and organisation and their subsequent elaborations in bio-political powers. Of course, what Fanon also teaches us is that these grids of knowledge and power were initially developed in extra-European spaces where it was colonisation that set in movement the global formation of the modern world.

Such considerations alert us to geography and place, to the crooked distribution of powers and the spatial exercise of knowledge. Any object, monument, or museum, just like any memory or history, is caught and suspended in these networks. It is also in this tempo-spatiality that the works of postcolonial artists acquire their critical edge. The art and aesthetics that emerges is not simply the symptom of this manner of thinking and perceiving the world. It does not merely drag into view and earshot the previously occluded, forgotten, and negated: the return of the repressed, colonial world in the coordinates of the present. The challenge of this art lies precisely in its willingness to engage with the colonising heritage itself, with its languages, technologies, aesthetics, and ethics, with its art, rerouting them through the altogether more disturbing spaces and places of a modernity that has never been simply authorised by Europe. In the repetition that dubs the past to mark the difference in the present, the postcolonial artwork elaborates a critical cut across and within an inherited Occidental art discourse. Disassembling and reassembling the languages and techniques of what is transmitted as art, together with its accompanying critical grammar, the drive for the pleasure of the new is pushed out of joint, sent sidewards into an unacknowledged setting where the presumed autonomy of art and aesthetics suddenly becomes a pressing ethical and political issue. This interrupts a deadening historicism and its order with the agonism of time in which the past refuses to pass, is not yet past, and occupies our time attending a reply.[17]

A SLASH IN TIME

The materiality of things—wood, stone, paint, metal—can be made to stand out and interrupt the flow of the quotidian. They can acquires a prophetic reach and suggest that we think again and push our minds and lives into unsuspected territories.[18] Looking through the mundane towards something else, feeling in the situation another untapped dimension, is to be exposed within one's culture to both its limits—always ready to dismiss the unexpected and cancel the uninvited—and its potential for renewal. Here perhaps it is necessary to lower one's eyes, reduce the objectifying gaze that reconfirms the sovereignty of my subjectivity, and enter a process that is simultaneously provocative and pedagogical.

If many of the pieces in the Cherokee artist Jimmie Durham's creative lexicon are seemingly natural in origin, they are staged and worked in such a fashion as to strip away any immediate appeal to the romanticism of both nature and the figure of the artist. Stark in their statements, unyielding in their materiality, such works draw us into a space that cleaves apart a merely anthropocentric framing of life and its forces. They leave a cut, a gap, an interval. The wood, the stone, assembled and linked, are never merely natural objects, just as the metal and the paint are not simply dumb witnesses to human and industrial production. They form a language. They speak of a situation and bring into play coordinates that we are accustomed to holding apart. Matter out of place—the replicas of bones and animals covered in acrylic paint scatted among oil drums and automobile parts—makes connections that we would never have made.[19] Such an art is not only critical in its invitation to thought but also profoundly political. With the latter term I intend an ethical imperative that carries us beyond the obvious exercise of existing political organisations into a conversation with the coordinates of a terrestrial condition.

This is to unravel the categories we are accustomed to deploy. It renders us slightly homeless. It weakens the drive to decipher it all. The illusion of clarity is substituted by a challenging opacity in which nothing is fully resolved, all is in a state of becoming. This is to be brought to earth, to tread an altogether rougher ground than that provided by abstract values and the reification of our lives in goods and capital and their endorsement of so much of contemporary art. It is to explore the spaces in the net that seemingly sustains us and consider something more, something else. Here Jimmie Durham the artist, poet, and writer who has been ethnographically objectified and marginalised—as the vanishing Indian and Native American—becomes the traveling ethnographer who presently resides in Berlin and Naples. Our desire for authenticity in art and ethnicity is disavowed. The splinters of that suffocating image, or burden of representation, are reassembled into another telling. We are invested with the culture we believe that we know so well—modernity, nature, and their classification, distinctions and definitions by the social and natural sciences—as it comes to be transformed into a seemingly illegitimate trail of interrogations. What, after all, should be restricted to the realm of anthropology insists on being art. It refuses to be captured and colonised by the category prepared for it. The Native American trespasser in the white rooms of the gallery casts a disquieting interrogation. The neutrality of the edifice is brusquely exposed as a place of exclusion, its desired order daubed by an uncontrolled hand. If this can sometimes still be sustained in the seeming exotic purchase of an art that lies on the threshold between ethnography and aesthetics (for example, Aboriginal dot paintings of ancestral dreaming from the Australian desert that resonate with modernist abstractionism), Durham's work does not permit this form of accommodation.

The material that 'contains intensely meanings / Which it can no longer pour out' maintains its questioning spirit even in the slick scenes of the art world hustle.[20] These are memories—and here Jimmie Durham's work elicits a potential rendezvous with that of the German artist Anselm Kiefer—seared into the insistent materiality of the world.[21] Both artists create holes in history, not through an act of disembodied creation but by changing the objects and making connections that impel us to look again and to be drawn to participate in a memory and a history we have avoided or denied.[22] The undoing of any simple Native American or German 'identity' is enacted through the material becoming an interrogation. There is no immediate picture or proposal but rather an opening in the fabric of our lives that permits us to travel to its dark interiors to see what has been cast away and there gain a wider freedom. Beyond this suggestive loop, Durham's work forces us to confront the authenticity of the inauthentic; that is, the desire for the pristine moment and its unsullied expression always instigates the copy of a copy that seemingly returns us to the primal scene. What becomes authentic at this point is not a fetishised object or person already framed and formed in a catalogue of definitions, but rather the performative instance. It is the latter that conjoins the coming together of histories, cultures, and beings in a non-prescribed arrangement of life whose very alterity with respect to the consensual numbing of difference proposes a slash in time. In this unwinding of the sources of ethnographic stability, the other is no longer secured in a fixed place to be exhibited and explained, but rather becomes a subjective singularity among others. What we might hope to see in Jimmie Durham's art turns out to be a broken mirror whose shards can never be reassembled into a previous state that reflects us or the idealised other. Our theories and feelings are forced to travel; in transit they lose their initial purpose to dominate and define. They become traces in an altogether wider and unfolding complexity.

We now find ourselves in an archival space that has little to do with monumentality and much to do with artistic practices and ethical instances that uproot the drive for stable definitions and facile catalogues. The presumed continuity of time and explanation that docks in my explanation here slips out of hand into the wider contingencies that sustain me and the language I think I own and command. The concentration of explanation in 'my' world transmutes into an unsuspected eccentricity where meanings are multiplied, creolised and follow other, altogether more dynamic and unstable, maps.[23] Such an interference is neither simply to be located at the local or at the global level. The shift is altogether more seismic. It registers the necessary dismantling of inherited coordinates and the renegotiation of what location and belonging come to mean in a world that is neither homogeneous nor a uniform field of diverse forces and actors. In others words, the culture and history that nominated and defined art, its protagonists, practices and participants cannot simply be adjusted to incorporate what was previously ignored, repressed or dispatched to the margins, there to be labelled native, indigenous, exotic, and primitive. What is at stake here, relayed in both aesthetics and ethics, is the contestation and dismantling of the relations of power that permitted that previous state of affairs to rest hegemonic.

While the borders—between Europe and the rest of the world—continue to be exercised they are also increasingly crossed, confuted and mixed into a political economy that incorporates the art world but does not necessarily ever fully digest it. Something is always destined to live on and survive as troubling supplement and potential refusal. This is not an argument about agitprop or documentary realism; it is rather to suggest that the agonism inherent in the practices of contemporary art move within coordinates that necessarily unravel any aesthetic that cleaves to an ahistorical measure of the beautiful and a subjective rationalisation of the sublime. The world is an altogether wider, wilder, and less accommodating space when the so-called margins fold in on the presumed centre creating new fault lines, shifting landscapes, unplanned trajectories.[24]

The question of the relationship between reality and representation falls apart as the stability of a unique measure unravels. Images and imaginations now emerge in transit, transformation, and translation.[25] They can never be brought back to a single source or explanation. Postcolonial art works to denude that particular hold on the world. It seeks to establish a cultural discontinuity, and from there rework what is ultimately the colonial archive and its constitution of the present into another space and temporality. This is to tear ourselves away from the comforting continuities proposed by a Hegelian historicism of dialectical development and chronological progress. It is to understand, as the Italian feminist art critic Carla Lonzi argued many decades ago, that only a critical relationship to the present permits connections to a past that would otherwise remain unintelligible.[26]

Against the moribund order of time enveloped in institutional history, the critical order of contemporary emotional life and stimuli provoked by gender, sexuality, and race interrupt the neutral pretensions of the former. To recognise and reorder the discourse is insufficient, for it fails to acknowledge the powers (patriarchal, racist) that historically legitimated its languages and knowledge. Rather, commencing from the 'failure' of history and sociology to fully explain the processes and relations that they apparently understand—the narration that never gets it right and so has continually to be retold—we can tap into another space. If history authorises certain archives and not others, then the insistence of the 'unexpected subject' (Carla Lonzi) fractures time with the proposal of what has been excluded from its disciplinary premises and temporalities: women, sexual minorities, non-whites and non-Europeans.[27] This is to nominate histories still to be written, archives still to be registered. It is to insist on an experimental knowledge, a history in the making that explores the passage between representation and repression as a temporal and epistemological break. More than most practices, postcolonial art alerts us to this possibility and promise.

AFRICA AS MODERNITY

At this point, listening to the contemporary Iraqi oud player Naseer Shamma playing the ninth-century compositions of Abu l-Hasan 'Ali Ibn Nafi, better known as Zíryáb, we are drawn into a mutable geography of memory (and forgetting). Meaningful details are dynamically drawn from the past into the intensities of the present becoming future.[28] Here the sounds of an archive, of a deeper history, disturb and interrupt the codification of historical time as the privileged site of a universal rationality whose simultaneous point of departure and arrival is Occidental reason. These micro-tonalities, composed by a ninth-century cosmopolitan Muslim dandy, who travelled from Baghdad to Cordova, spill out of the Arab oud into sub-Saharan Africa. They resonate across the Atlantic, via the black diaspora induced by the racist slave trade, to reverberate in the blue notes of subaltern cultures and their music making in the Americas.

> In broad terms it would seem that the practice of embellishment and therefore very often of fluctuations and 'bends' in the notes becomes steadily more marked as one moves through the savannah regions to the desert. Perhaps it is the Arabic influence that determines this; or perhaps it is an outcome of the greater use of bowed string instruments which may both rival and stimulate the use of the voice. Certainly the ornamentation of the Tuaregs reaches a degree of enrichment that exceeds any in the blues and comes very close to that of *cante honde* and *flamenco*. In the singing of many of the parkland and semi-desert peoples the use of shadings and falling notes that approximate to those of the blues can be widely heard.[29]

In the interiors of the body of sound we discover folds in time that permit other times to be heard. Reasoning with sounds as living archives we encounter unsuspected genealogies, other modalities to rhyme, rhythm, and reason the world that ruffle and disturb the singularity of the approved narrative. Such sounds promote counter-histories. They disseminate intervals and interruptions in the well-tempered score which the hegemonic accounting plays to itself.

Let us remain in this space and consider Africa as the site of what Jean and John Comoroff have called 'Afromodernity'.[30] It is here that the colonial past emerges in our midst as an uninvited guest, casting a persistent shadow over the archive. The history of the modern south, constructed in the political economy of a planetary modernity to be colonised by the predatory capitalist concerns of Euro-America, now becomes an unsuspected space. Rather than a residual or underdeveloped place to where the material refuse and racist refusal of the modern world is directed, it becomes a critical site of interrogation and interruption in the very midst of a modernity that considers it to be merely marginalised.

This is not an archive simply to be mined and exploited, but rather one that is still to be registered; that is, to be acknowledged as a central component in the modernity that tends to exclude its presence in the narrative. If Africa is still presented as trying to catch up with the modern Occidental world, the arts of Africa, their travels and transformations, narrate another history. This is a history, relayed in contemporary sound and images, that draws us into mapping a very different set of itineraries crossing the formation of modernity. The point here is not only to disturb accredited historiographical tools of explanation and propose another modality of archiving and research sustained by the audio and visual arts. It is also to suggest a critical configuration that evidences the historical presence of Africa in European modernity as much as the usual tale of a colonial Europe in Africa. This is less about collating the historical evidence of Black Athena or pointing to the deep history of mankind's long march out of the Grand Rift Valley towards the rest of the world. Rather, and more urgently, it is to insist that modernity has always depended on planetary coordinates and coordination. Here, redrawing inherited geographies and historical pathologies, Africa emerges as a central element in its formation. This is to contest the externalisation and marginalisation of the non-European world in the making of modernity as a 'white myth' (Jacques Derrida).

These considerations can clearly be extended to contemporary African art. Here works exist along multiple scales that not only and most obviously confute such binary distinctions as the local and the global, but also prove impossible to be slotted into the categories prepared for their reception: African and authentic. African artistic practices subtract themselves from subordination to the categories of anthropology and sociology where they are expected to confirm Occidental perspectives. Today, this desire is consistently dissimulated. An artist such as Yinka Shonibare MBE, who ironically insists on his paradoxical historical membership of the British Empire in his very name, deliberately reworks the past of Europe in Africa while conjoining it to the present of Africa in Europe. Recovering, replaying and redressing the past in this manner evades simple accommodation or fixed locations. The historical and cultural fluxes proposed by such work crosses the art world with histories of complex narratives. These speak of multiple belongings. The heterogeneous assemblage of materials and icons in Shonibare MBE's works—Dutch colonial wax prints, West African couture, British naval heroes, the *Ancien Regime* and Victoriana—queries the cultural construction of a consensual aesthetics when the materials of empire are reworked into another narrative.[31] Against the predictable lineage of Occidental art history an altogether more complex and undisciplined archive overflows the frame, proposing a supplement that cannot be readily accommodated or incorporated.

Such art proposes less an object to be analysed and explained according to the logics and languages of artistic and disciplinary canons and more a critical *dispositif* or apparatus with which to think, live, cross and interrogate a discursive regime that thinks it is able to explain and render art an object. In this scene, the past with its memories and archives proposes a diverse genealogy and a different modality for receiving its presence in the present. There is no pure or isolated object, nor a definitive explanation of the past, to be discovered. Rather, there are historical and cultural processes to be acknowledged. This marks the critical passage, of Foucauldian memory, from registering the strata of archaeology to arriving at a productive genealogy.[32] It proposes breaks and discontinuities; that is, a working of the past into new critical configurations. There is no pristine past to be discovered, but rather the tracing of processes where what counts is not the object that is unearthed but rather the processes that constitute both it and the manner of its unearthing.

This suggests that rather than simply tracking Africa in Europe, it becomes urgent to think *with* Africa. Here Africa is retrieved from being an object of analysis and research as it becomes an emergent critical space, an ongoing interrogation and interruption. This is rather beautifully captured in Abderrahmane Sissiko's cinematic enactment of the hypothetical trial of the IMF for holding modern Africa hostage to debt in *Bamako* (2006). With this we step beyond the colonial division of the world that has only considered Europe in Africa, and never of the constitutive role of Africa in Europe. Moving beyond such binaries is to suggest a critical space in which the existing cartographies of power are disassembled and remixed in an economy of signs and sounds that challenge the conceptual confines of Occidental art history and its critical language.

This deviation is not set in train simply in order to recognise alternative and subaltern realities. Initially, this may be important and necessary, but it is a point of departure, not of arrival. To travel further into the question is to register the worlds that have persisted and resisted within modernity from its inception as part and parcel of its global web. Unrecognised and negated, Africa in Europe, like the black slave in the history of capitalism, or colonial troops deployed in Europe's imperial wars, is a constant shadow interrogating the modernity that consigns them to its margins. These are realities whose presence have not simply been repressed and are now being belatedly recognised. Rather, their historical and cultural centrality to the making of a modernity we consider 'ours' forces us to rework the archive that once authorised us; that is, to break it open and spill its contents into further critical contours and other tellings of the world.

At this point the limits and location of the European narrative is sustained, as Olu Oguibe puts it, in the 'divergent historical trajectories that constitute a colonial or postcolonial modernity'.[33] Here it becomes imperative to 'read within the frames of a larger historical moment'.[34] This means to measure the terms of participation in modern art and modernity, rather than being simply incorporated or co-opted as an external and exotic 'other'. It further means to inaugurate breaking the spell of Occidental legitimation for, as Rasheed Araeen puts it: the 'structure of colonialism cannot be dealt with only by those who are colonised'.[35] This leads to the necessary unwinding of the history of art as a liberal, humanist Occidental discourse which has historically and culturally contributed to the elaboration of the colonial apparatuses that also legitimated its voice and authority.

The absence of contemporary African art in Occidental institutions is therefore not simply the symptom of a colonial pathology that continues to think of Africa as 'down there and back there', and desires only the anthropological authenticity of local African arts and crafts. For what it poses is a hole in the epistemological fabric that clothes the West, and it is one that cannot simply be patched up with threads drawn from existing disciplinary protocols. This would only be a further colonial move. The idea that an artist or curator working in Lagos or Luanda moves and is sustained in the material and immaterial circuits that constitute the international art world is still rarely considered. Of course, he or she operates within unequal relations of cultural power and recognition: Lagos is not Los Angeles, Luanda is not London. Still, connections and a potential resonance are undeniably in play. There simply does not exist a shadowy exterior cast by the light of Occidental progress. The sounds and images of James Brown in Mali in the 1960s, and their unsuspected conversations with local youth styles and photography, is far less about obvious U.S. cultural imperialism in the so-called underdeveloped world and altogether much more about multiple connections to black diasporic aesthetics both after European colonialism and beyond local post-independent nationalism.[36] If Africa has always been part of the historical constitution of modernity, it has also been inside the cultural and aesthetic networks of its modernism. Alongside the noted art history narrative of Cubism and Surrealism sampling the continent we now begin to touch the deeper economy of the circulation and translation of ideas, perspectives and practices that never move in a single direction nor respect rigid centre-periphery distinctions.

NOTES

1. The Palermo performance is no longer available online. Another live performance by Mike Cooper of the same song, recorded in Reading, England, in 2009 is available at https://www.youtube.com/watch?v=uWWcQ73j-hE.
2. Ricœur 2006, 79
3. Moten 2003.
4. Gilroy 1993.
5. Le Goff 1992, xvii.
6. Le Goff 1992, xix.
7. Le Goff 1992, xix.
8. Zaatari 2013.
9. Rabinow 2007.
10. Diagne 2013.
11. MacDonald 2008.
12. Ricœur 2006, 79.
13. Ricœur 2006, xvi.
14. Didi-Huberman 2000.
15. Ricœur 2006, 89
16. Deleuze 2006.
17. Benjamin 1969.

18. Durham, "Wood, Stone and Friends", Exhibition at Palazzo Reale, Naples, December 15, 2012–February 27, 2013.
19. Durham, "Traces and Shiny Evidence", Exhibition at Parasol unit, London, June 12–August 9, 2014, http://parasol-unit.org/jimmie-durham-traces-and-shiny-evidence.
20. Durham 1994, 58.
21. For an overview of Kiefer's work, see https://www.royalacademy.org.uk/exhibition/anselm-kiefer.
22. Durham 1994, 70.
23. Hassan and Oguibe 2002.
24. Tawadros and Campbell 2003.
25. Lusini 2013, 110.
26. Zapperi 2015.
27. Curti 2017. For a significant example of such an archive, composed by contemporary women artists in the Mediterranean, see the website of MatriArchive of the Mediterranean at http://www.matriarchiviomediterraneo.org.
28. Shamma 2003.
29. Oliver 2001, 61–62.
30. Comaroff and Comaroff 2012.
31. For examples of Shonibare's work, see http://www.yinkashonibarembe.com/home/.
32. Revel 2010.
33. Oguibe 2005, 419.
34. Oguibe 2005, 420.
35. Araeen 2005.
36. Diawara 2001.

Chapter Six

Folds in Time

Let me begin by considering this statement from the Indian historian Partha Chatterjee:

> People can only imagine themselves in empty homogeneous time; they do not live in it. Empty homogeneous time is the utopian time of capital. Its linearity connects past, present and future, creating the possibility for all of those historicist imaginings of identity, nationhood, progress, and so on that Anderson, along with others, have made familiar to us. But empty homogeneous time is not located anywhere in real space—it is utopian. The real space of modern life consists of heterotopia.[1]

These incisive words clearly evoke the voices and thought of Walter Benjamin and Michel Foucault. They draw us into considering a modernity that is not simply doubled by subaltern actors and forces seeking to contest the hegemonic version of a history that insists on a unique telling. As the Haitian anthropologist Michel-Ralph Trouillot reminds us, archives are never merely given nor fixed; they are always agonistic practices and institutions: 'Archives assemble'.[2] Recognising the intersecting and planetary distribution of difference, location, and singularity there emerges an understanding of modernity that is disseminated in shifting rhythms along multiple scales within combinations of heterogeneous powers and practices. Against the empty dream of an utopian alternative permitting withdrawal from the seemingly unavoidable impositions of actuality, the heterotopic perspective proposes that we step out of an existing version of time to drop deeper into the folds of the contemporary world; there to assay and absorb its potentialities. Here, time is split from itself to permit the registration of other temporalities producing other spaces. An imposed and seemingly inevitable futurity is marked by the return of other, unacknowledged times. No longer the victim of a rigid archive, confined to the predictable rhythms of a numbing tradition, the past here becomes a vibrant t/issue that interrupts the present. The legitimated combination of materials comes undone, the archive is shaken apart and its documents, voices, objects, and silences scattered over altogether more contingent maps. Set to diverse patterns and imperatives, the past comes to be configured by present urgencies in an emergent critical space. In this sense, the present is still in the making: understandings have not yet jelled; they are still under way, open to contestation, redirection and reformulation.

CUTTING THE CONTINUUM

To step sideways, and remove oneself from the implacable logic of a unilaterally conceived modernity, is to step out of the frame of an abstract temporality. As a conscious incision, an alternative take, a blue note and deliberate dissonance, the idea of heterotopic thought and practices seeks to burrow below both the topographical logic of Foucault's disciplined spaces and the eternal dialectic of narrative and counter-narrative. If we could consider remix as a method, just like jazz improvisations on the 'standards', or the unhomely melody of the blues, or the DJ's 'cut', then we can confront and configure the sedimented and intersectional composition of a modernity that does not move to a single beat or uniform pulse. In this form of historical and cultural reasoning we are encouraged to think more in terms of shifting combinations and unsuspected resonances that draw on the techniques of repetition and dub, rather than remain locked in the power of established positions contesting and dividing the singularity of sense. The historical conjuncture is ultimately a performative space elaborated along multiple planes, diverse trajectories, and unpredictable depths. The *ratio* is neither linear nor transparent.

This leads us to consider interruptions and discontinuities as a historical method. Slices in time expose the sedimentation and cross-fertilisation of different rhythms and localities sounding out and performing the historical present. Slices in time: that is intervals in the narratives, interruptions in the machinery of truth. For Foucault's heterotopia suggests far more than simply registering the question of a differentiated spatiality and acknowledging the unregistered volume of the contemporary world.[3] To cut space up into a multiplying assemblage is also to conjoin time in diverse rhythms and temporal instances. The desire to represent modernity as the perfect match of linear time and stable, homogeneous space is thwarted; that kind of geography now falls apart. This teaches us that critical labour is not simply about contesting the imposed temporalities of hegemonic rationalities. Rather, it is also about constructing spaces based on another sense of time; here the reconfiguration of the present releases a further set of spatiotemporal coordinates, and another manner of reasoning. What now returns to the map is what was excluded by the premises of the previous cartography of power, of knowledge. This operation, like a Deleuzian 'fold', creases and deepens spatiality while rendering diverse temporalities proximate. It produces the interleaving of heterogeneous dimensions that resonate with the circulation of bodies, lives, histories, and cultures in what we now come to understand as a manifold modernity.

In this sense, as Foucault insisted in the Preface to *The Order of Things* (1966), the heterotopic instance breaks through and beyond the homogeneous order of a discourse. Heterotopia proposes the elision of the imposed. Language and space no longer match: the former is unable to contain and control the latter. The map is no longer reality, merely a restricted representation. It is at this point that the limits of the epistemological device—the map, the discipline, institutional knowledge—promote an ontological rift. For if utopias are the product of language, heterotopias are manufactured and maintained in the mutable materialities of space where language seeks to impose its temporal order. If utopias by their very nature do not exist, they are nevertheless cultivated and cared for in language and discourse. Heterotopias, on the contrary, even if unregistered and unrecognised, do exist. They, too, require language and are therefore not without their utopian drive, but they sustain diverse experiences of inhabiting history and culture, different practices of time and space.

Alternative, subaltern, and subordinated to the rules that occlude their presence, heterotopias exist and persist as counter-spaces beside and beyond the consensual syntax of sense. Their presence uproots the premises of the linguistic and discursive order, proposing a flight and a freedom from its imposition. They propose a disturbance, an intimation of the uprooted and a homelessness with respect to the security offered by the previous order. If space is produced (Henri Lefebvre) and never simply given, it is not simply produced by our language. It is construed, constructed, crossed, and signified by many different bodies (and not all of them human). This heterogenetic understanding of the spaces and temporalities of the modern world is clearly irreducible to the mirror of Occidental concerns and conceit. The actors and agency involved are not merely of European provenance. The 'world picture' (Heidegger), proposed by European humanism, and secured in the historical expansion and cultural domination of capitalism and colonialism, no longer (as if it ever did) provides a seamless fit between representation and reality. What once lay outside the frame has entered the picture, traverses and troubles the perspective. The field of vision, the map of the world, turns out to be a contested field in which borders and belongings are increasingly fluid, tactical and transitory; hence the increased application of violence—both physical and juridical—in seeking to control and direct them.

No doubt such comments stretch and even desert Foucault's original discussion of heterotopia by pushing 'experiments of the self and the social' out into the exposed spaces and temporalities of the postcolonial world. Still, this return to Foucault in an altogether more extensive landscape also allows us to pick up further items from his *oeuvre* that clearly continue to vibrate in contemporary critical circuits. Here, confronting a global order produced by Occidental culture and capitalism, Foucault's attention to the productive relations of power, to differentiated bodies and their government, provide important critical levers for reopening that vault. Where power is the power to exploit subordinated bodies and extract wealth by conquest and dispossession, then the genealogy of 'progress', and the associated modernity of European culture and its accompanying anthropologies, sociologies, histories and institutions are exposed as regional inventions. Of course, these locatable practices often continue to disavow the historical, cultural, and geo-political coordinates of their production. The rest of the world is forcibly conscripted to that modernity, and there consistently subordinated in order to be exploited, catalogued, or even cast overboard or exterminated; everywhere reduced to the deadly calculus of objectified value in the abstract circuits of capital. This is not a moral judgement, but a structural and historical one. It proposes not simply a timeless ethical horizon, but also, and more insistently, a precise political one.

... AND CROSSING BORDERS

Maps, as Sandro Mezzadra and Brett Neilson have effectively pointed out, are epistemological devices of profound ontological significance.[4] In their modern history, which is not by chance the history of European expansion on a planetary scale, maps are pictures of power, representations of rule. They establish not simply territory and property, but also cognitive confines that seek to locate and control bodies and cultures both at home and abroad. Further, given that such rigid spatial distinctions are increasingly redundant, they insistently chart and remap the flows and fluxes of tangible and intangible mobilities on multiple scales, from immediate localities to the planetary. In this history power is masked in maps, murder is presented as measurement, and genocide becomes geometry. Cartography becomes the transposition of the violence of the commodity form into the implacable territorial 'laws' of the world market.

The power to map, mould, modify, and morph reveals the architecture of power: it is never simply the application of a technical, neutral or 'scientific' language. In border zones, such as that between Israel and the Occupied Territories, it has promoted a set of social and historical practices that lead to what Eyal Weizman calls a 'laboratory of the extreme' producing a 'dynamic morphology of the frontier'.[5] The territory, Weizman continues, is never as flat as a map, but striated beneath our feet (aquifers, land rights) and above our heads (air corridors, electromagnetic waves full of radio signals, cellular phone networks, GPS positioning, wide band computer communications). With Ilan Pappé justly referring us to Israel as the ultimate settler colony, disenfranchising the local Palestine population through an apartheid regime, the situation there actually turns out to be exemplary rather than exceptional.[6] This is to touch the imperial hubris of the West and the discomfort of other settler colonial societies—one here has only to think of the United States (or Australia, New Zealand, and Canada)—having to condemn the very practices that produced their sovereignty. Meanwhile, similar procedures scan the Mediterranean, just as they patrol the U.S.-Mexico border. Maps are multiple, simultaneously vertical and horizontal. They produce a continually mutating three-dimensional matrix. Flexible, mobile distinctions sustain invisible lines and shifting zones of material and immaterial territory, labour, wealth, and their subsequent management. As distinct frontiers slip into oscillating border zones they are never simply physical nor static. They are rather flexible instances of authority that sustain the continual production of interleaved borderscapes. The assumed modality of reaching out from the centre to control the periphery via the imposition of a unique power and authority now gives way to the flexibility of an altogether more diffuse molecular management. The patrolling and profiling of the planet promotes a new experiential and conceptual landscape, together with their affective economies. This invites us to consider how the order of power is inscribed and articulated, emerges, and reproduces, itself in a multidimensional temporal space.

Whether violently imposed or subtlty inserted into the circuits of our lives, borders as mechanisms of power are also critically and culturally productive. The border is a framing device that gives transitory shape and sense to both what it contains and what it seeks to exclude. If the border ushers in an instance of the exceptional state—where each and every one of us finds his or her status and citizenship temporally suspended before being reconfirmed (or challenged)—it reveals, in the diffuse intensity of its bio-politics the underlying protocols that define and confine its own domestic populations. Borders force us to reconsider the historical, political, and cultural configurations that gave rise to their presumed necessity. They bring back into the picture what they were previously designed to exclude: the defeated, the subaltern, the other histories and territories of belonging that push up against this seemingly impassable framing. If politically rigid and legally slow to mutate, borders are culturally fluid and socially multifarious: for some they represent merely stamps on a passport, for others an apparently impossible barrier, yet every day they continue to be crossed in legal and illegal fashion, and hence are simultaneously challenged and confirmed.

From the particular and dramatic instances of Tijuana, Juarez, El Paso or Quetta as border cities we are propelled into thinking the whole world as a multiplicity of border zones, traversed by legislation, enforcement and bureaucracy, and then complicated by the unaccounted histories and cultures embodied in their being increasingly crossed by clandestine bodies. Most obviously, we encounter this situation and its arbitrary violence in the southwest deserts of the United States, along the northern edges of the Sahara and on the waters of the Mediterranean Sea, on both sides of the English Channel, in the ambivalent territories of Palestine and Kurdistan, between South Africa and sub-Saharan Africa, or Asia and Australia in the Timor Sea. It is all too easy to forget that these borders also run through the streets, languages, arrangements, and divisions of First World cities. The multi-ethnic populations of Los Angeles, London, and Paris are also researched, profiled, and policed. For even if these populations are certainly resident *in* the nation they are frequently considered to be not be fully part *of* the nation. As has been noted, the externally exercised bio-politics of yesterday's colonial administration, so sharply analysed by Frantz Fanon and reproposed in Gillo Pontecorvo's *Battle of Algiers* (1966), has not so much disappeared as transmuted into the technologically sustained, and hence altogether more flexible, management of the modern political body of the Occidental metropolis.

BLOCKS AND BREAKDOWNS

Following Chatterjee, this suggests the necessity to break with a manner of narrating time and space as though from a homogeneous point of view: Europe, the West and its accompanying mapping of knowledge (historical, sociological, anthropological, and economic—in sum, the constellation of the human and social sciences). In a planetary political economy of knowledge, those sciences that have largely disciplined and explained the world cannot be cancelled; but they can be reworked in response to altogether more extensive maps. The methods that apparently guaranteed universality, once placed in the specific historical and cultural formation of modern Europe, are exposed to interruption and interrogation by 'foreign' forces, voices, and relations. Borders are contested and crossed, disciplines interrupted, languages retuned. Of course, the power of this inherited assemblage is formidable. Practised and institutionalised on an increasing world scale, over centuries of military, political, economic, and cultural domination, this form of knowledge and its claims to universal validity remains hegemonic.

As was suggested at the beginning of this book, present-day academic labour, refereed journals, national research assessments and global university rankings all testify to the presumed 'neutrality' of this precise exercise of power. Yet it is ultimately a deadly mechanism, able only to rationalise once it has 'killed' and objectified the foreign body, the extraneous event. It analyses in a manner that reduces the complexity of life to the confines of the discipline, to the parameters of the recognisable, transforming the opacity it pretends to explain into a moribund transparency, shunning vital ambiguities for the still life of an abstract verdict. As a knowledge formation it privileges the protocols of its reproduction over engagement with what precedes and exceeds its ken. Ultimately, despite detailed description and verifications, it opts for the comfort of conclusion rather than the disquiet of a critical departure and accompanying vulnerability. Knowledge is reduced to the procedures and protocols of the accredited method and the consensual paradigm. What is sought is a homecoming rather than the journey, self-confirmation and not exposure to the unplanned encounter.

What, then, are these other forms of knowledge? Where and how are we to locate these unrecognised epistemologies of modernity? Insisting on the idea of heterotopia, is to insist on understandings, knowledge formations and practices that may well be marginalised and yet exist and resist. They persist besides us as a part of the modernity we consider our own. If we were to employ a Freudian topography, they would constitute the sedimented layers of modernity's unconscious. Perhaps a more horizontal topology better illustrates the unrecognised heteronomies of modernity. The critical knowledges that emerge in the dynamics and mutations of a planetary modernity can no longer be considered simply the provenance of the psychically repressed and physically distant. What was once dismissed in the peripheries of the world can no longer be relegated to the posterior conclusions of discarded colonial maps. Today, Occidental governance has to work much harder to block other forms of knowledge entering the picture and disturbing the narrative frame. Of course, the world continues to be ruled from that particular house of knowledge, but then it is hardly a critical knowledge, rather more an administrative security hubris that seeks to reproduce itself and, as a consequence, the dynamics it commands. Yet lived, the present acquires flesh and follows multiple directions. Its sense is neither merely inherited nor imposed. Transformed into the urgencies of a body, a life, a location, the transit of modernity reveals the centrality of translation, and a world that persists without single or unique approval.

MARITIME CRITICISM

In his conclusion to his brief comments on heterotopia, Foucault famously nominates the ship as one of its privileged sites. The ship, the sea, slaves, rebels, and castaways, together with the whole archive of Caribbean poetics (Édouard Glissant, Derek Walcott. Maysée Condée, Michele Cliff, Edward Kamau Braithwaite, Bob Marley, Lee 'Scratch' Perry), alerts us to a decisively alternative manner of crossing and configuring modernity. For attempts to politically and juridically 'fix' and frame the sea according to the requirements of terrestrial coordinates always go adrift. It is the fruitful and suggestive critical nature of this 'drift' and its floating premises that most clearly invest us with a series of questions that are perhaps rarely posed. Here, and most obviously, the status of borders and confines are continually challenged by marine transit, migration (both legal and illegal), encounters with opacity, and an emerging sense of belonging to an extended and more fluid citizenship that is irreducible to the terms of the existing polity. The critical limits of a monopolising reason are well caught in the following observation from Dipesh Chakrabarty:

> For the point is not that Enlightenment rationalism is always unreasonable in itself but rather a matter of documenting how—through what historical process—its 'reason', which was not always self-evident to everyone, has been made to look 'obvious' far beyond the ground where it originated.[7]

Commencing from the maritime world, rather than the habitual location of land and territory, is clearly to propose a destabilising style of argument in which unknown factors, critical uncertainty and ungrounded anxieties are foregrounded. Such a choice of perspective has much to do with deliberately seeking to unsettle many of the disciplinary procedures and protocols of the social and human sciences. Opposed to dreams of systematic order and the assurance of canonical convictions to be accommodated in libraries, museums, data-bases, school and university syllabuses, what we might call 'maritime criticism' sets existing knowledge afloat: not to drown or cancel it, but rather to expose it to unsuspected winds and currents. The presumed stability of the historical archive, together with its associated 'facts' and cultural beneficiaries, invariably sealed in the narration of the nation, becomes susceptible to drift, unplanned contacts, even shipwreck. As we have learnt from the rebellious maritime world of the modern Atlantic, suspended in its depths, there exist histories and cultures that are connected, rather than divided, by water. In that 'grey vault, the sea' (Derek Walcott) there lie other ways of narrating both a local and planetary modernity.

Choosing to return to this liquid domain is not merely a metaphorical whim. The sea has been consistently central to the making of Occidental modernity. Voyages of so-called discovery, European colonisation and the global nets of imperialism, have all been about the sea: mapping it, crossing it to colonise other worlds, controlling it to conquer global hegemony, traveling its sea-lanes in the pursuit of the reorganisation of planetary labour (from yesterday's slave ship to today's container vessel), harvesting its resources (from fish and whales to oil and gas). Rarely, however, has it been considered in its own right as an ontological challenge to the histories and events that apparently require terrestrial grounding in order to be narrated. Yet the politics and poetics of the Caribbean archipelago of creolising histories repeated and reworked from island to island, together with the subterranean circuits sustained in the base cultures of the black Atlantic diaspora sounding Africa off against Europe and America, suggest an altogether different telling of the tale.

The intensity of historical negation and the political energies deployed in the repression of such counter-histories produces a series of gaps and holes in the heart of the progress that modernity supposedly embodies. Through racial discrimination claims of democracy fall apart in the refusal to permit its exercise in the lives and labour of others. Only a teleological acceptance of historical progress can confidently claim that this earlier state of affairs has finally been overcome. An understanding attentive to the genealogies of the contemporary structures of exploitative power in Occidental modernity would be altogether less assured. We remain facing the sedimented and structural articulation of a particular arrangement of power, privilege and its perpetuation. Haiti disappears into this black hole (politically quarantined and historically cancelled by the West throughout much of its history, just like Cuba since 1959), allowed only to appear in the alien alterity of abject poverty and voodoo. Meanwhile, subterranean appropriations of the political and cultural language of modernity, orbiting around questions of freedom, liberty, and universal rights, disseminate critical questions that connect the eighteenth-century Atlantic world to the modern Mediterranean. Both slaves in Caribbean revolt and modern migrants seeking to improve their lives and enter 'Fortress Europe' tend to be considered illegitimate intruders in the narrative. It is precisely here that the maritime archive sustains another accounting of modernity, casting a critical wave into the contemporary mechanisms of controlling and defining Europe, the Mediterranean and the modern world.

French and British sea-borne empires fighting for global hegemony simultaneously in the eighteenth-century Caribbean and the Mediterranean propose a 'global colonial archive' that continues to haunt the present.[8] Nelson in the Bay of Naples crushes the Neapolitan Republic (inspired by the French Revolution and hence sharing unexplored coordinates with the rebellion of Wolfe Tone's United Irishmen and the 'Black Jacobins' in the contemporary slave rebellion in Saint-Domingue). The previous year he was in Egyptian waters at Abu Qir Bay (the so-called Battle of the Nile) destroying the French fleet that had transported Napoleon and his troops to Egypt to seize this Ottoman province, thereby initiating the future European construction of the Middle East. Here shifting surfaces, islands, currents, and depths of the marine world offer a critical interruption, an exit from the linearity of the technological conquest of space and an associated historical narrative that unfolds in the empty abstraction of universal time seemingly secured in fixed terrestrial coordinates.

If today's Mediterranean has clearly become the maritime cemetery of modern day migrant life, it simultaneously proposes a liquid archive that draws us back to the watery recesses of the modernity we think we know so well. Beneath the waves, on the other side of the official chart, are anonymous processes and peoples making the modern world from below, from 'way, way below'.[9] It is these clandestine histories that sign the unsuspected register of a heterotopic modernity: one that is irreducible to a single perspective or unilateral geo-political framing of the planet. As Ranajit Guha suggestively puts it: 'since Columbus, Europe had been obsessively engaged in voyages of self-discovery requiring it to try and match the coordinates of intercontinental space by those of universal time—geography by history'.[10]

SOUNDS AND INTERRUPTIONS

The fluid archives provoked by maritime criticism, and the maps of modernity traced by the black diaspora and modern migration, suggest a historiography of not how things actually were, as though forever fixed in time and secured in terrestrial and scientific 'objectivity', but rather of how things are, exist, survive, and live on. Here there are artefacts, documents, material traces, but there are no historical 'facts' isolated from the human and social activity of appropriation and interpretation. The present is haunted and interrogated by the past. The dead continue to speak in the insistence of images—visual, scriptural, acoustic—loaded with time. A linear historicism snaps and unravels. This is to work with the proposal of an interrupted and interrupting history, a history of intervals and discontinuities, of multiple temporalities.

Out of the traces of time other configurations emerge to promote a diverse narration of both yesterday and today. Such memories of the future, as we know after Freud, and so evocatively traced by Chris Marker in his film *Sans Soleil* (1983), are indivisible from the media that record them. They propose other historical records. The prevalent historical discourse is crossed by the insistence that history, precisely because it is always pertinent, always now, is not simply a matter that can be left to echo in the institutional archive and its appointed historians. What history and whose history is irreducible to a neutral catalogue of the past. The official tale is always lined with other memories: personal, collective, incomplete, and imagined. These memories, whether recalled or consigned to oblivion, are also where illegal passages and clandestine tellings seek alternative narratives of belonging and becoming. This, as Ranajit Guha points out, is to recover and subsequently subvert the Hegelian concept of the 'prose of the world' by insisting on its right to query the philosophical privileging of the 'prose of history' embodied in the modern European nation state.[11] The transformation of the negative identification of a 'people without history' into a positive critical injunction is precisely where the extra-European world becomes an interrogative and historical force *within* a modernity that presumed its necessary exteriority.

Alongside a supposedly factual economy, and its conclusive empiricism, is an *affective* one that discovers itself in inconclusive interpretations, and which seeks its rigour in the complexity of the historical locality and cultural constellation in which it moves. Faced with this irreducible complexity the key of interpretation lies in critical honesty rather than the illusory neutrality of objectivity. It is precisely at this point that the postcolonial artwork insists not merely as testimony to a historical past and present, but rather in terms of provoking a diverse configuration of time, being, and becoming. We are not dealing with aesthetic ornaments to add to the cruel drama of historical and cultural formations. Details and fragments—shafts of condensed time—sustained in artistic languages, in a poetics, propose, as both Walter Benjamin and Aby Warburg argued, another and radically different way of understanding and interpreting such formations. This is what the artist and critic Bracha Ettinger calls *artworking*.[12]

Music, the visual arts, poetry, literature, even recipes, are neither merely metaphorical nor symbolical. In their material affects and through their undisciplined reach, such languages become critical. They are able to disturb and displace the authority of the disciplinary accounts provided by the narrow concerns of historiography, sociology, anthropology, art history and literary criticism. At this point, the image—whether visual, textual, or auditory—is less the object and attention of thought and more the instigator of thinking. From the detail, the fragment of condensed time, from the dynamics of an image, the dissemination of sound, it becomes possible to rethink a space: the Mediterranean, Europe, modernity, the contemporary world. Against the desire for conclusive transparency, there is an indisciplined overflow whose reach promotes a poetics and a further, unsuspected, politics. Such an interval opens on to a critical space that runs through, alongside and beyond the immediate pragmatics of a regimented time and place.

Between the black histories of the Atlantic and the contemporary Mediterranean we can therefore also chart an ecology of rhythms, beats and tonalities that lead to sonic cartographies where, as Steve Goodman has put it, 'sound comes to the rescue of thought'.[13] Drawn from a blue archive that plays and replays modernity, exploiting the spaces between its official notes, unsuspected sounds and combinations cross, contaminate, and creolise the landscape. Such musical maps provoke forms of interference that render hidden histories and negated genealogies audible, sounding them out and rendering them sensible. Sounds matter. They also propose and extend critical matters. They acquire a narrative force that draw us towards what survives and lives on as a cultural and historical resource able to resist, disturb, interrogate and fracture the presumed 'unity' of the present. Music promotes the alterity of official time, subtracting us from its implacable seriality it promotes subjectivities that overstep the rules and rites of representation.[14]

To think of the Mediterranean in terms of acoustic sustenance, leading to an unsuspected deepening and dispersal of the empirical present, is to embrace what Gilles Deleuze and Félix Guattari would have called a 'minor' history. This is to tear existing cartographies. It returns us to what has been overlooked and unheard, and permits other stories and unsuspected spaces to emerge. If established powers refuse to listen, as they inevitably do, then these sounds trace another, largely unrecognised, projection that shadows and potentially interrupts the seamless surface of consensual understanding. Here, considering the Mediterranean as an 'infinity of traces without . . . an inventory' (Antonio Gramsci), sonic histories propose a persistent 'noise' that disrupts the institutional silence of the historical register. Sounds become a source of critical disturbance, and the musical archive 'a question of the future itself, the question of a response, of a promise and of a responsibility, for tomorrow'.[15]

Like the sea, that often facilitated their passage, sonic processes resist representation and linguistic limits to propose an affective economy, 'stripped of consolation and security'.[16] They are inherently diasporic, destined to disturb fixed configurations of time, space and belonging while being involved in sounding out communities to come. Against a stereotypical image, Mediterranean sounds, as they travel, disseminate and differentiate, propose a complex cultural and historical place that can be heard in a diverse and altogether more open manner. This, for example, is what the Palestinian critic Edward Said came across in his adult rediscovery of the voice of Umm Kalthūm.[17] Trained in the well-tempered aesthetics and classical musical seriality of the modern West, the lengthy improvised vocals of the Egyptian singer initially seemed to him as if it were a sound on the edge of critical nonsense. Subsequently repositioning himself in and to the West, and hence to the voice of the excluded other, Said drew from this unsettling experience the suggestive perspective of a multiple and *contrapuntal* modernity.

Thus, to respond to the voice of Umm Kalthūm is not merely to recover a sonic signature from the negated archive of Mediterranean musical memories, it is also to propose another critical compass. Her voice and music were not simply that of a particular Arabic musical and poetical tradition. The manner of her singing and the execution of her music were also profoundly modern. If her voice, with its extended melodic lines, shifting intonations, *melisma* and the privileging of the performative, obviously draws upon a long history of improvised musical execution in the Arab world and elsewhere (European classical music is here the exception rather than the rule), it also resonates profoundly with other modern, improvised metropolitan sounds of the twentieth century: above all, with the music of the black diaspora, with the blues and jazz. Although largely unknown and unheard in the West, the music of modern, metropolitan Cairo between the 1940s and the 1960s is the sound of Umm Kalthūm. It is not the 'traditional' sound of a folk music, antecedent to a subsequent entrance into modernity.

Umm Kalthūm was musically and culturally very much an innovative figure and a modern woman. Regularly transmitted on the radio, ceaselessly recorded, and presented in innumerable public concerts, she was a popular and commercial 'star', and a persistent public presence in the Arab world.[18] Kalthūm's musical existence in the modern Mediterranean suggests an unsuspected proximity with other sounds, other places, other histories, that the altogether more strictly confined understandings of musical and cultural identification has structurally failed to acknowledge. This Mediterranean, as a complex cultural and historical formation, presents us with a 'unity in difference', where, as the musicologist Bruno Nettl notes, the challenge of heterogeneity is nevertheless characterised by certain common traits: for example, the ubiquity of certain percussive and plucked instruments (from the oud and the guitar to the mandolin and the bouzouki), or the strong imprint of Muslim music making with its modal systems and monophonic structures.

Gilles Léothaud and Bernard Lortat-Jacob have pointed to the musical centrality of a fluid East-West axis that marginalises the rigidity of the classical north-south division between a modern, Christian, Europe and an underdeveloped, Islamic world.[19] They argue that the Mediterranean 'voice'—in the hint of a cry (think of Arabic song, flamenco, Neapolitan vocals and Greek rebetika), in its nasal intonation, in its dark, rough and granular textures, in the insistence of *melisma* rather than a distinct punctuation, in the voice on the edge, close to breakdown—registers the exertion of the body in the song, and resonates in the ear as a distinctive Mediterranean musicality. Opposed to the rigidity of many institutional explanations and the insistence of the securities of local and national myth, the fluidity of sounds proposes an altogether more frayed and fluctuating map. It allows us to consider how the multiple histories of the Mediterranean are suspended and sustained as instances in time that render its complex and ongoing configuration momentarily audible.

Here the question of 'art', no longer secured in terms of aesthetic autonomy, historical mimesis and cultural representation, restores the body to its multiple senses. Such a recovery of sensory geographies provokes a consideration of music in terms of a sensuous epistemology that touches on other, subaltern and suppressed, knowledges. These are carried in the body, sustained in sound, registered in rhythm, broadcast in the persistence of a 'bass history' from below.[20] We are here engaging with an altogether more diffuse and less instrumental epistemology than that associated with the objectifying procedures of sight and the accompanying fetish of truth as representation. Thought is here installed by sound.

The renouncement of reducing music to an object of historical, sociological, and cultural definition brings us to reflect on the production of bodies through sounds. In other words, we are not here considering subjects that encounter sounds, but rather engaging with subjectivities configured in sound. Music at this point does not 'represent' a pre-existing state but rather promotes a sensual and social becoming. Sounds and musical practices alert us to a potential and irreversible breakdown in representation: the sound floats free and disseminates an unsuspected critical challenge. A particular manner of singing or playing does not simply represent the cultural concerns and historical insistence of a precise community, social group or subculture. It does not simply do that. The sound is dispossessed. If music inevitably contributes to the cultural and historical tuning of the world it traverses, the fluidity and the differentiated immanence of its passage is also irreducible to a single moment of cultural legitimacy. In this sense, the sociology of music is displaced by music as sociology. Sounds do not so much illustrate as propose histories. They narrate and affect an attachment to a memory, a place, a trace. They elaborate a temporary territory, a transitory home in the world.

This, as Julian Henriques has rightly suggested, leads to shaking 'the monopoly of rationality and representation'.[21] To consider music as proposing the potential of unsuspected areas of sense, secured in what is felt rather than fully explained, is also to challenge ideas of identities that seemingly root and resume the sound. In the prospect of a concentrated affectivity of materialities, sound, performance, reception, and repetition tend towards unsuspected, more vulnerable and more open, critical instances. This reasoning in the archive of repetition, brings us into proximity with the concept in Arab music of *tarab*: the ecstasy or enrapture that results from the stretching of vibrations through a reiteration that is never the same, that continually unfolds in becoming the song and the sound. Opposed to the isolated, individual achievement of abstract musical perfection, the performative possibilities of improvisation include the audience as it strives towards the creation of community. In the repetition lies the temporary autonomy of a territory sustained in the event of sound where music promotes a reasoning medium. Here where 'time is split from time' (A.J. Racy), music does not 'mirror' or 'communicate' a seemingly separate and independent reality, it is itself a form of reasoning, rather than a representation.[22] As such it participates in a history of the discontinuous, always disturbing the imposed teleology of modern historical time.

UNCHARTED WATERS

We have travelled with the ontological challenge of the sea to the critical cut of sound. Both evoke an interruption that propels us beyond the securities of domestic imperatives and deliver us into another space. The news that arrives from the sea and musical interruptions in representational reason provokes the freedom for critical piracy. It becomes possible to raid and retreat from the home of thinking grounded in the provincial immediacies of a unique locale and language. This suggests an idea of history profoundly indebted to Walter Benjamin and his *Theses on the Philosophy of History*. Here knowledge, sustained by the search for new beginnings, proposes history not from a stable point of origin, but via a movement in which the historian emerges not as the source but as the subject who can never fully command nor comprehend his or her language. In a similar key, anthropology and sociology become the objects of their own disciplinary gaze:

> On close examination, mainstream sociology turns out to be an ethnosociology of metropolitan society. This is concealed by its language especially the framing of its theories as universal propositions or universal tools.[23]

We are called upon to navigate in languages, currents and conditions not of our own making. This is the post-human confirmation that what we see does not commence from the eye, but from the external light of the world that strikes it. It means to engage with a history composed of intervals, irruptions and interruptions. While utopia promises eventual consolation in the emptiness of a time yet to come, the heterotopic promotes the critical immediacy of a disturbance, sustained in the diffusion of tempos, rhythms, and spaces that mark the multiplications of modernity and snap the links of a singular understanding. There is no space—of modernity, of identity, of history—without other spaces, without the spaces of others. This is a form of knowledge, one should say a political proposal, that refuses to be aligned with a unique and unilateral understanding. It crosses the spaces of academia and institutional authorities without being inherent to them; it is itself heterotopic, always alongside, besides, and hence beyond, the point.

Undoing the Hegelian inheritance of the presumed match between European history and reason, whereby the history of the world is synonymous with the 'reason of history' (Ranajit Guha), is to chart the implications—critical, historical, political—of the complex uncoupling of modernity from Europe.[24] It is to chart modernity and its tempo-spatial coordinates on an unfolding planetary chart of entangled histories. If Europe without its 'other' is inconceivable then it is that relationship, which since 1500 has acquired sense in its global extension and intimacies, and not a particular location or 'source' that provides the critical matrix. Thinking with these wider coordinates it then becomes a question not of others catching up, developing and mimicking a European measure of the world, but rather of understanding the historical and cultural centrality of that repressed and refused world to the making of Europe and the modernity it presumes to own and represent. To transform this repressed relationship into a measure of Europe is to draw critical rigour from what exceeds its languages of knowledge and power.

This, to return to the Hegelian inheritance, is to propose a history that does not simply accommodate what previously was rejected and ignored. It is rather to transpose a localised, European inheritance into another space, signified in the planetary premises of the colonial configuration of the globe. In other words, this is not a historical modernity that emanates through waves of progress outwards from the metropolis towards the periphery, drawing the latter into its development. It is rather a constellation or network, composed of shifting nuclei and relations in which distanced cultures and events can resonate in unsuspected proximities: revolution in Paris, the slave revolt in Haiti and philosophical pronouncements on the master-slave dialectic in Berlin; the principles of perspective, algebra, the mathematical meaning of nothing (zero) and their transmission via the Arab world to the foundations of Italian and European humanism. It is to consider those silent holes in the web of planetary modernity; the holes that sustain the mesh.

If this all leads into a territory characterised by what Gurminder Bhambra in *Rethinking Modernity* calls 'connected histories', it also drops us into unsuspected and uncharted waters.[25] Learning to float, rather than seeking immediately to drop anchor, is to accept exposure to a world that is not merely ours to legitimate. Charting this space, the prevailing topologies of power, formed in the exploitative flows of existing economic, political and cultural life, can be cut to reveal disturbing discontinuities. Here the heterotopic is not only about a withdrawal from everyday life (the prison, the asylum, and all their critical negativities), but also about the deepening and extension of its possibilities (the journey, vulnerability, exposure, trans-disciplinarily, and trans-national knowledge). This cut or exit does not lead to an 'outside', but rather to another contemporaneity. It remains 'within' the materialisation of planetary possibilities, proposing 'lines of flight' and 'dub' versions of consensual reality. If culture today is increasingly disciplined by the dynamism of economic valuation, the seeming transparency of this self-referring bubble floats in a space where it is also unable to sense what escapes and exceeds its algorithms. There continue to exist alternative accountings of the world that threaten to unplug the digital data bank, crack the screen and twist the existing rhizomes of power into the multiplicities of the post-colonial city and the multifarious spatio-temporalities of a planetary communality that is not only capitalist in intent and extent.

This is to suggest a worldly modernity that is always under way, susceptible to other winds and currents. Opting to travel in an uprooted modernity that can claim no unique source or singular history is to propose further critical beginnings.

ANOTHER MEDITERRANEAN

At this point, and to reference my own personal location in southern Italy, I find myself considering a diverse manner of inhabiting, receiving, and understanding the Mediterranean. Another way of telling requires a narrative style able, if not to encompass, at least to register an excess of sense that spills beyond reductive rationalisms, nationalisms and the disciplinary confines of existing knowledge. To permit the Mediterranean to float into other accounts is both to extend and deepen its configuration and to pull it away from the pretence of an exhaustive telling. This inevitably provokes critical engagement with the disciplines, institutions, and authorities that have given rise to modern explanations of the Mediterranean.

No single definition or spatial confinement can contain what we are seeking to talk about. Present-day European borders stretch way across the Mediterranean and deep into North Africa. Not only are foodstuffs destined for European markets grown according to standards established by EU legislation, but the thousands of migrant deaths in the Sahara and the Mediterranean Sea are also directly attributable to European law. As a commercial, political, and juridical space, the Mediterranean, and its European-dominated definition, is mobilised along invisible frontiers thousands of kilometres southward and eastward from its shorelines.

Ferdinand Braudel continually pointed out that the Mediterranean has always been sustained and suspended in wider networks. These considerations suggest the adoption of mobile and multiple frames of reference for understanding its continual composition. If the attempt to introduce more disruptive currents into the consideration of its past—for example, Martin Bernal's *Black Athena*—have hardly dented disciplinary defences, the insistence of creolised cultural configurations and hybridised historical formations of the Mediterranean nevertheless persist and resist. In food, taste, language, sound and music other cartographies are sustained. They suggest a mixing of histories related to altogether more extensive geographies. Tomatoes from Peru and coffee from Ethiopia are part of a culinary cartography that proposes travel on a far wider axis than that assumed by European definitions of the composition of the present-day Mediterranean. Such geographies propose a complex and multi-scalar sense of belonging. They breach those offered by the apparent stability of existing localisms, nationalisms, and their institutional definitions.

Rather than a single space to be studied, the Mediterranean—as an area in-between Europe, Asia, and Africa—becomes an interleaved and multistratified configuration, a point of dispersion and dissemination rather than a single, concentrated unity. Yannis Hamilakis, referring to the exclusive pretensions of modern Western archaeology, calls this 'alternative engagements with materiality and temporality'.[26] This means to propose multiple and diverse archaeologies where Egypt, Greece, and Palestine do not exist simply as ancient Egypt, Greece, and Palestine. They cannot be reduced to the Pharaohs, Hellenism, and the land of the Bible; restricted to representing monumental, and now superseded, moments in the subsequent development of European civilisation. They are not merely the mirror of Europe's historical past and contemporary progress, which recovers that past largely in order to measure itself against it. In this parable, the intervening centuries of Arab, Ottoman and Balkan histories and cultures are reduced to a deviation or unfortunate parenthesis to be expunged. This permits the eastern Mediterranean to be thoroughly Europeanised, and the continuities and contemporary impact of Islam, Arab culture, and the Ottoman Empire, overruled. To return those histories to the picture carries us well beyond a structural adjustment; it inaugurates a radical reconfiguration of the history (and culture) that presumes it is best able to tell the tale, define the Mediterranean, manage its archives, its archaeologies, and propose its meanings.

The materiality of memory—those sounds, flavours, and tastes sustained in linguistic, musical, and culinary arrangements, for example—suggests a Mediterranean that defies any obvious genealogy. The past that survives and lives on in these languages, frequently ignored, refused and reduced to the cultural marginalia of the established historical archive, actually registers a diverse type of historical recollection. Altogether more ragged, modest, and incomplete, these are memories that proposes a past, which, as Nietzsche put it, cannot be dissolved into pure knowledge.[27] Cultural and artistic perspectives register time and space, sustaining localities, archives, and memories, that simultaneously deepen and extend the sense of the past as a connective medium, bringing together in their differences a mobile communality and potential conviviality.

Weaving languages together into multiple conversations it becomes possible to dub and disturb dominant rhythms and figures. The musicality of narrative, of memory, their accents and intervals, resonances and dissonance, crack the collusions of the seamless tale of existing powers. The complexity of a layered set of languages and aesthetics proposes a diverse style of remembering, and a redistribution in shifting historical and political landscapes, as they come to be sedimented and inscribed in the construction of the archive. Here a conventional historical and geographical map of the Mediterranean, operating along the bi-dimensional plane of sensorial indifference, can be torn and creased; it can be folded into other, unsuspected accountings and testimonies of time to produce further critical spaces. Such memories promote a poetics that in turn leads to a very different politics.

This other power, stemming from minor histories and subaltern cartographies, does not merely confuse and confute the existing picture, but actually sets the terms for another map and a further unplanned geography of a Mediterranean still to be acknowledged and received. Here we come to touch the limits of inherited narrative apparatuses. The performative power of memory promotes an archive whose coordinates may initially coincide with, but ultimately confute, the established referents.

Considering cinema as a means of memory, we can commence a conversation with Michael Haneke's film *Caché* (2005). A repressed and negated presence—Algeria—irrupts in the daily fabric of modern-day Paris. Within the shared coordinates of a colonialism that united France and Algeria, the film promotes the unwinding of history under the impact of anonymous missives from a colonial past that refuses to pass. The wound remains open, unattended, ready to infect the present. The regular beat of everyday Parisian bourgeois life is interrupted, pushed out of synch, reversed and crossed by other rhythms and voices unable to find accommodation in the accepted score. We are invited to consider who is looking at whom: the familiar gaze—under Western eyes—is challenged by those refusing to accept the cultural and historical destiny of that ocular logic. We, too, are observed, rendered objects in a world where the once colonised insists on the right to be a (postcolonial) subject. The West finds itself exposed in the anonymous gaze of objectification under the eyes of a negated colonial past and present. Knowledge, a memory (filtered, censured, forgotten, denied) of the place of Algeria (and colonialism) in the making of modern France (and Europe) becomes the site of an interruption. As a cut through which other times emerge, the film insists on the ordinary, everyday textures and sentiments of this negated and unconscious dimension of modernity. Declaring he has 'nothing to hide', the Parisian protagonist consistently avoids the unacknowledged history that would undo his assured command of the present. Narrative time, however, like the anonymous videocassettes arriving on his doorstep, can be reversed to recall the past. The linear logic that insists on the single and homogeneous order of the present, history as the chronological passage of temporality, is cut up, slowed down, intensified and fixed in a frame, to announce another montage of the modern world. Here, to affront the question of time—whose, where, why, and how?—is to consider the possibility of its consensual flow and direction being deviated and disrupted. Cutting up time in this manner, we encounter all the powers and interrogations of what Derek Gregory aptly calls the colonial present.[28]

SEDIMENTS, FOLDS, RUINS, AND RHYTHMS

To abandon the abstract blocks of time of conventional linear history and an associated geometrical space, means to distil time and space into the sociality of a continuum perceived in intervals, interruptions, and rhythmic constellations as they configure the present.[29] The force of rhythm propels us into thinking the material movement of bodies and cultures in time and space that sets the abstract in thought to follow another pulse. To consider the Mediterranean (and modernity) in the logic of such intervals is, once again, to insist on slicing up the continuum of time and space into singularities disseminated in the rhythmic imperatives of different localities and their diverse urgencies. If rhythm is about a regulated movement, it is clearly of an order separate from the linear flatness produced by the ocular and spatial organisation of chronologies and maps. Rhythms can change. They pick up further accents, grow emphatic and fade away. Rhythm promotes a constant return that engenders difference. Rhythm is of the body, of the historical body, of the history that produces the body and in turn is appropriated by that body. Again, Stuart Hall helps us to understand the historical and cultural costs of negating this ongoing formation:

> Since the Sixteenth Century, these differential temporalities and histories have been irrevocably and violently yoked together. This certainly does not mean that they were ever or are the same. Their grossly unequal trajectories, which formed the very ground of political antagonism and cultural resistance, have nevertheless been impossible to disentangle, conceptualise or narrate as discrete entities: though this is precisely what the dominant western historiographical tradition has often tried to do.[30]

Listening to the intensities of historical and cultural configurations, where multiple elements are brought into play, is not to make an argument about a perpetual state or essence of the Mediterranean. It is, rather, to insist on a radically diverse accounting of time and space; one that is most obviously pre- and post-national in abjuring established geopolitical entities. It is also one that insists on heterotopic understandings that respond to diverse emphases and beats. To insist on a history that seeks its sources in the rhythms of the Mediterranean is not to seek a secret centre that scores the narration. Rather is to register a polyrhythmic coming together that grounds, provokes, and promotes multiple and individual voicing. We are not looking for an organising principle but a process of dissemination, not a conceptual rule but a critical reverberation. It is the latter that is potentially able to host the diversity of the unsuspected. The former can only impose itself through refusing the disturbance of elements that interrupt its tunes and taxonomies.

This challenges the violence of the prevalent logic of space and frontiers. The prevalent flattening of space and the unilateral management of time serves to confirm precise locations that are the objects of exploitation, surveillance, protection, policing, and the provincial promotion of political and disciplinary identities. The threat of poly-vocal heterogeneity is rejected in the name of an implacable logic secured in the nation, the West, and their subsidiary mechanisms of knowledge. Of course, we know that these traditions are all contaminated, none of their concepts and practices have developed in isolation. They all depend on being split between their self and an other: they are all products of intercultural translations and historical transit, none autonomous or 'pure'. Just as Christianity is so deeply imbricated in the genealogy of the two other monotheisms of Judaism and Islam as to be a variant, so the West without the rest collapses as a conceptual space.

A multilateral Mediterranean, irreducible to European history and geography, points to another critical space. If the European I/eye can clearly no longer speak for, or in the name of, its other shores, it can nevertheless take an apprenticeship in learning to speak in the vicinity of an African and Asian Mediterranean. The historical narrative and European framing that seemingly sets the terms for past and present understandings, from Fernand Braudel to David Abulafia, can be interrupted.[31] The teleology of an explanatory unfolding in time and space under the banner of European 'progress' (but who defines that very loaded term?) can be deviated and set within another set of coordinates. Engaging with European explanation it is also possible to propose voices, bodies, and histories that such an explanation has structurally marginalised and consistently sought to rob of authority. Islamic, Arab, and Turkish histories and cultures as components of both the Mediterranean and Europe—of its cultural, religious, and political life—are invariably reduced to culinary details and musical inflections, minor footnotes in the epic of Occidental development.

We still move within a European-derived history that remains largely oblivious to the critique of its historicism. Despite the disturbing noises that arrive from the archive, history continues to be sourced in the security of continuity. To abandon the prevalent historical narrative in the gardens of historicism, annotating time and registering 'progress', and to lean into the margins is to catch the whiff of counter-historiographies. Surely, today it is impossible to pretend to narrate the past, to explore the archive, to mine memory, after Nietzsche and Freud, after Gramsci and Benjamin, after Derrida and Foucault, as though we are dealing with dead objects to be grasped and revealed in the seemingly neutral language of a knowledge—'history'— guaranteed by the scholarly protocols of the human and social 'sciences'. All of these terms—history, human, archive, memory, social, science—are critical, susceptible to interrogation, interruption, contestation, and reconfiguration.

If we take David Abulafia's *The Great Sea: A Human History of the Mediterranean*, we confront a six-hundred-page opus that moves from the dawn of human records to the present. Here we might provocatively ask, how is it possible to concentrate almost exclusively on the European shore while studiously avoiding how Europe produced and managed the Mediterranean's spatiotemporal syntax?[32] Operating with the universalising grammar of disciplinary 'neutrality' to set the record straight and sustain a teleological narrative, an abstract idea of 'human' history remains immune to such problematic understandings of modernity as colonialism, imperialism, modern nation-state formations, and the constitution of the discourses of 'history' and the 'human'. The implication, despite the density and complexities of empirical detail, is ultimately that of reconfirming the status quo in which geopolitics are translated into historical predicates, and vice versa.[33]

The struggle for hegemony in recent centuries in the Mediterranean (just what was Nelson doing in the Bay of Naples in 1799, or in Egyptian waters at the Battle of Abu Qir a year previously?) alerts us to the planetary coordinates that transformed the Mediterranean into a colonial theatre and a European lake: from Marrakech to Damascus, the African and Asian shores and hinterlands were ruled from Paris, London, and Rome. When Shelomo Dov Goitein refers to Fustat (now incorporated into modern day Cairo), the twelfth-century Fatimid capital of Egypt located on the Nile some two hundred kilometres from the sea, as the hub of a medieval 'Mediterranean society', we can better grasp the potential critical shift.[34] There are few today who would immediately associate this Nile city with the Mediterranean. Insisting on Goitein's definition, and adding Janet Abu Lughod's analysis of the Eurasian mercantile system of the thirteenth century that orbited around such 'world' cities as Cairo and Baghdad, we puncture the pretensions of a unilateral European narrative.[35] The coeval presence of these other knowledges—their traces, testimonies, and transmission—complicate and multiply the official Mediterranean narrative. This is not simply a case of a forgotten or repressed past returning to haunt the present. It is not merely about a richer and more nuanced picture. To reopen the archive in this manner is not only to reorder and reassemble its materials; it is also to question the manner of its construction, the politics of its narration, and to interrogate the premises that disciplined its organisational will in the identification of voices, artefacts, documents, and materials, and the requisite repression of others. In other words, the archive is precisely not about dead matters. It is always under construction: what it informs us about the past (and hence the present) is frequently still to be registered and narrated in a responsibility for the future.

Rather than sweep the Mediterranean into a single, unified tale (ultimately that of European 'progress' and civilisation), it seems more instructive to consider a communality sustained in differences and discontinuities. Let us listen once again to the scholar of the unintended Jewish archive of medieval Fustat, Shelomo Goitein. Drawing on the more than a quarter of a million documents abandoned in the storeroom or Geniza of the Fustat synagogue between the eleventh and thirteenth centuries, he writes:

> The people speaking to us through our documents represent an intrinsically urban population. Their world comprised urban sites from Samarkand in central Asia and the port cities of India and Indonesia to the east, to Seville in Spain and Sijilmāsa in Morocco to the west; from Aden in the south, to Constantinople, the capital of Byzantium in the north. The maritime cities of the northern shore of the Mediterranean, such as Narbonne, Marseilles, Genoa, Pisa, and Venice, are also mentioned in the Geniza records and were indeed visited at the end of the twelfth century by Jewish traders, whose letters home are preserved in the Geniza. There are sporadic references to faraway European places, such as Rouen, the capital of Normandy in northern France, and Kiev in the present-day Ukraine. It is, however, the Islamic city of the Middle Ages that is most clearly reflected in our documents.[36]

Within the modern Mediterranean there are countless examples of such extended, inter-cultural networks characterising both place and belonging. In his detailed historical account of the city of Salonica under the Ottomans (1430–1925) and beyond to 1950, Mark Mazower writes of the concentrated microcosm of Mediterranean monotheisms—those religions of the desert (Judaism, Christianity, and Islam) that developed in trans-cultural diffusion—while considering the history of Salonica in a montage of intertwined narratives that speak of breaks, blocks, and oblivion.[37] The narrative of *Salonica. City of Ghosts. Christians, Muslims and Jews 1430–1950* concludes in the present-day Greek city of Thessaloniki. Here we encounter the engineered undoing and cancellation of the cultural, historical, political, and religious composition of Ottoman urbanity through the violent impositions of Hellenic nationalism aided and abetted by fascism. If in 1925 the Muslim population was 'exchanged' with the Greek one in Anatolia, in 1943–1945 the Nazis then exterminated the sixty thousand Sephardic Jewish population in the death camps of Central Europe. The importance, however, beyond the terrible cost of ethnic cleansing and the drive for national homogeneity, lies, as the title of Mazower's book reminds us, with the ghosts. Here the refusal to remember is registered as being as important as the official insistence on historical precedence and preservation. As Freud understood when visiting Rome, such sites of memory and sedimentation render our premises vulnerable precisely through the presence of the negated, the repressed, the silenced.

This form of contemporaneity, the joining of past and present in a critical configuration, does not avoid the evidence of the archive, or pretend to render it transparent, but rather reworks and revitalises it. The importance of the histories proposed by Goitein and Mazower is that they reverberate along multiple scales and dimensions. Localising and folding time and space into discontinuous complexities, they do not pretend that the world can be laid out as flat as a map and there conclusively catalogued. The latter manner of archiving and its associated archaeology is invariably accompanied by the persistent policing of identity politics, of both those in dominance and those subordinated to domination in the categories of ethnic, cultural, religious, and linguistic 'minorities'. If the existing narrative accommodates this dialectic of asymmetrical powers it clearly cannot offer hospitality to the idea that its very terms and premises need to be set on altogether more transitory (that is, *historical*) foundations. In *The Venture of Islam*, this is precisely what Marshall Hodgson proposed to undertake in analysing what he called Islamicate histories and cultures.[38] There he sought to unhook Western history 'from Eurocentric teleologies' and apply to both the world of Islam and to the Occident the Gramscian directive to think in worldly terms.[39]

The histories of the eastern Mediterranean under Islamic hegemony that have been swept under the carpet, relegated to the so-called Dark and Middle Ages, are not recuperated simply in order to fill the void that lies between the fall of the Roman Empire and the emergence of modern Europe. It is not simply about setting the record straight. What is proposed is an interrogation that epistemologically challenges the assumed superiority of the West over the rest. Set down on a wider and overlapping set of maps, respective provincialisms are exposed to questions that loosen them from secure moorings, requiring them to renegotiate their authority. Islamic culture, even in its supposed heyday, was not merely Arabic. Berber, Persian, and Turkish were also major components in its cosmopolitan formation. And if the thirteenth-century urban Islamic world of western Asia was eventually overrun by pastoral nomads (the Mongols) who then stayed on to be absorbed, the then contemporary European Renaissance did not inaugurate modernity but rather signalled the ingression of the outer region of the Afro-Eurasian landmass into the cultural complexity and sophistication of the larger cultura constellation of the *Oecumene*. To entertain what Hodgson argues is to operate a critical interval and interrogation in the Occidental design of progress. It is to consider the formation of modernity, both past and present, as an intertwined planetary phenomenon irrespective of its assumed 'origins' in Europe and the West. If paper, the compass, gunpowder, the decimal system, algebra, and the crucial figure of zero came from elsewhere, we are required to draw upon more extensive maps for our understanding. Similarly, ancient Greek thought, itself not separate from Asia and Africa, from Persia and Egypt, was recovered, resurrected, and then transmitted—and in the process transformed and 'modernised'—to the Occident from the Orient and the world of Islam. This is not to suppress the West but to complicate it, exposing it to a wider, less parochial series of understandings, located in altogether more extensive historical and cultural networks.

Finally, we are invested by the harsh reverberations of a world that runs on altogether rougher ground, beyond the rationalising desires of our will and the seamless pretensions of our knowledge. This suggests other ways of knowing, other powers sustained in other bodies and locales that reconfigure the modern condition in a manner that does not merely mirror our own understanding. This is to move within a space whose temporality is neither singular nor merely the registration of a uniform space. Time comes undone, spirals back on itself, splits into the coeval instances of representation and repression: the past lives on, ghosting the present, setting it to rhythms composed in continual interrogations. Out of time, and out of joint with respect to an imperious linearity, such tempos, intervals and improvisations sustain the space of histories yet to come.

Critical work now finds itself inscribing the limits of its premises and perspectives in an unruly world that never merely mirrors you or me. If we continue to interrogate, it is precisely because we are aware of the politics and practices of our position. Uneven powers and arbitrary violence cross and cut up the maps. The terrain they supposedly represent is treacherous to transparency, for it also houses other lives and narratives. The archives we construct are necessarily incomplete, broken with respect to a colonial desire that seeks its confirmation in every corner of the planet. As a set of ruins they justly expose us to a world not only of our making. Moving amongst the debris we are neither prisoners nor simply free. Sustained and suspended in a historical web that has woven the planet into a particular configuration of powers, we can nevertheless insist on other trajectories. The world is still in the making. There is no comforting horizon here, only the struggle to signify and secure a justice to come.

FROM A SMALL ISLAND

I would like to conclude at this point, in the company of the Ethiopian film maker Dagmawi Yimer and his film *Asmat* (2015).[40] Yimer, who presently lives and works in Italy, illegally crossed the Mediterranean to the island of Lampedusa and is presently a member of the Migrant Memories Archives collective in Rome.[41] His work has consistently orbited around the question of the contemporary migrant's condition which, as I have been trying to suggest, carries us into the heart of modernity itself. In his video *Asmat*, the Tigrinya for names, we hear the steady intonation of the list of the dead, of those, who were unsuccessful in their crossing, being rescued from anonymity. The names are visibly etched in water. They float as a series of question marks. Why this death, why this destiny for lost lives? The film offers no explanation. It is not a documentary. Its testimony lies more in the aesthetics of the abject. We are drawn in to listen and look, but can never completely understand or fully grasp the cruel materiality of the event. It evades reduction to a single point of view (mine, ours, the West) while wider coordinates of possible understanding, involving other histories, cultures, languages and lives, float into view. What is projected and portrayed are cyphers, names, from a world registered only in the statistics of death and drowning at sea: the mute objects of European policy and legislation. One can protest that the initial 'push' to migrate and be caught in the dangerous meshes of Occidental border control and legislation lies elsewhere. It is not our responsibility. But the violence, repression and blocked futures of North and sub-Saharan Africa, and further afield in Syria, in Afghanistan, in Latin America, draws us into deeper historical time. It draws us into a political economy in which our responsibility for the colonial making of the present reemerges with a dramatic immediacy. The entanglement of political, cultural, economic, and historical narratives exceeds the frame and the categories that justify our explanation and political definitions of the present. The abstract categories of the 'illegal' and the linear legislation of time—what we call history and progress—unwind, stripped of their authority in a planetary complexity that exceeds their claims.

The ethical and aesthetic affect of Dagmawi Yimer's film is to disturb our understanding of the archive—our understanding of the past and the present—with unsolicited horizons and unwelcome questions. It is a work that refuses to bear the burden of representing the migrant as simply a nameless, subaltern body, an authentic 'other', an excluded victim of the not yet modern world. Its horrible beauty requires us to listen to what has been silenced, rendered mute, removed from the accounting of time and place. For the migrant with her or his name and history is the modern world in all of its terrible consequences. It is this undoing and redoing of time, its doubling and dispersal with respect to a unique measure and explanation, that ensures the emergence of a new and amplified critical space.

The dynamics of the archive shift from the conservation and linear accumulation that benchmarks progress to redistribution and reconfiguration. In the latter situation we will inevitably encounter languages that do not necessarily reply to our needs. Against the abstract violence of representing a unique past—the national narrative, the museum display, the approved textbook—the archive breaks down. Here an emerging citizenship insists on the rights of memory to cross, contest and cut up legitimised explanations. Here the archive no longer contains the past, and with it our present and the future, but rather distributes an excess that propels us beyond the categories prepared for us. We are compelled finally to recognise that our citizenship—however restricted and disciplined it has increasingly becomes—structurally depends, both yesterday and today, on the colonial disposition of maintaining the vast majority of the world in a state of non-citizenship and unfreedom. Here we can begin to think the unthinkable. Over the border, in the souths of the world, the epistemological paradigm of the social and human sciences as Occidental property goes astray. They are betrayed in transit, in translation. They are potentially liberated and renegotiated as the asymmetrical relations of power that sustain their authority are historically and culturally exposed. If the monopoly of what counts for knowledge and truth is now increasingly challenged, nothing is cancelled; all is reconfigured, reworked and rerouted in a series of responses and responsibilities that now exceed a single, privileged, locality.

NOTES

1. Chatterjee 2003, 166.
2. Trouillot 1995.
3. Foucault 1986.
4. Mezzadra and Neilson 2013.
5. Weizman 2007.
6. Pappé 2015. See also Rodinson 1973.
7. Chakrabarty 2007, 43.
8. Conelli 2012.
9. Kelley 1994, 1.
10. Guha 2003,12.
11. Guha 2003.
12. Ettinger 2006.
13. Goodman 2010, 82.
14. Hodgkinson, 2016.
15. Derrida 1998, 36.
16. Eshun 2007, 78.
17. Said 1992, 98.
18. Danielson 1997.
19. Léothaud and Lortat-Jacob 2000.
20. Johnson 1975.
21. Henriques 2011, 122.
22. Racy 2004, 9.
23. Connell 2007.
24. Bhambra 2009.
25. Bhambra 2009, 81.
26. Hamilakis 2011.
27. Nietzsche 1997.
28. Gregory 2004.
29. Gérardot 2007.
30. Hall 1996.
31. Braudel 1995; Abulafia 2011.
32. Abulafia 2011.
33. Sakai 2011.
34. Goitein 1999.
35. Abu-Lughod 1989.
36. Goitein 1999, 38–39.
37. Mazower 2005.
38. Hodgson 1977.
39. Burke 1993.
40. Yimer 2015.
41. See http://www.archiviomemoriemigranti.net/en.

Bibliography

Abulafia, David. 2011. *The Great Sea. A Human History of the Mediterranean*. London: Penguin.
Abu-Lughod, Janet L. 1989. *Before European Hegemony: The World System, A.D. 1250–1350*. Oxford: Oxford University Press.
Adorno, Theodor, and Max Horkheimer. 2016. *Dialectic of Enlightenment*. London and New York: Verso.
Afary, Janet, and Kevin B. Anderson. 2004. 'Revisiting Foucault and the Iranian Revolution'. *New Politics*. http://newpol.org/content/revisiting-foucault-and-iranian-revolution.
Agamben, Giorgio. 1998. *Homo Sacer: Sovereign Power and Bare Life*. Translated by Daniel Heller-Roazen. Stanford: Stanford University Press.
Agamben, Giorgio. [1993] 2000. *Means Without Ends: Notes on Politics*. Minneapolis: University of Minnesota Press.
Akomfrah, John. 2013. *The Stuart Hall Project*. London: BFI.
Alessandrini, Anthony. 2014. 'Foucault, Fanon, Intellectuals, Revolutions'. *Jadaliyya*. http://www.jadaliyya.com/pages/index/17154/foucault-fanon-intellectuals-revolutions.
Alioua, Mehdi. 2005. 'La migration transnationale des Africains sub-sahariens au Maghreb: l'exemple de l'étape marocaine'. *Maghreb-Machrek*, 37–58.
Althusser, Louis. 2001. 'Ideology and Ideological State Apparatuses (Notes Towards an Investigation)'. *Lenin and Philosophy and Other Essays*. New York: Monthly Review Press.
Amin, Ash. 2010. 'The Remainders of Race'. *Theory, Culture, Society* 27, no. 1: 315–332.
Amin, Ash. 2012. *Land of Strangers*, Oxford: Polity Press.
Araeen, Rasheed. 2005. 'Modernity, Modernism, and Africa's Place in the History of Art of our Age'. *Third Text* 19, no. 4: 411–417.
Arendt, Hannah. 1973. *The Origins of Totalitarianism*. New York: Harvest Books.
Ascione, Gennaro. 2016. *Science and the Decolonization of Social Theory. Unthinking Modernity*. London and New York: Palgrave Macmillan.
Ascione, Gennaro. 2017. 'Unthinking Capital: Conceptual and Terminological Landmarks'. *Sociology*, vol. 56, n. 1, 1–19.
Baldwin, James. 1963. *The Fire Next Time*. London: Penguin.
Baldwin, James. 1972. *No Name in the Street*. New York: Vintage.
Balibar, Étienne. 2008. 'Historical Dilemmas of Democracy and Their Contemporary Relevance for Citizenship'. *Rethinking Marxism* 20, no. 4: 522–538.
Balibar, Étienne. 2014. 'Hannah Arendt, the Right to Have Rights, and Civil Disobedience'. In *Equaliberty: Political Essays*. Durham: Duke University Press.
Baucom, Ian. 2005. *Specters of the Atlantic. Finance Capital, Slavery, and the Philosophy of History*. Durham: Duke University Press.

Bauman, Zygmunt. 1991. *Modernity and the Holocaust*. Oxford: Polity Press.
Belpoliti, Marco, and Robert Gordon, eds. 2001. *The Voice of Memory. Interviews 1961–1987*. Cambridge: Polity Press.
Belting, Hans. 2010. 'Afterthoughts on Alhazen's Visual Theory and Its Presence in the Pictorial Theory of Western Perspective'. In *Variantology 4. On Deep Time Relations of Arts, Sciences and Technologies in the Arabic-Islamic World and Beyond*, ed. Siegfried Zielinski and Eckhardt Fürlus. Cologne: Walter König.
Benhabib, Seyla. 2002. *The Claims of Culture: Equality and Diversity in the Global Era*. Princeton: Princeton University Press.
Benjamin, Walter. 1969. 'Theses on the Philosophy of History'. In *Illuminations and Reflections*. Translated by Harry Zohn, 253–264. New York: Schocken Books, 1969.
Benjamin, Walter. 1999. 'Critique of Violence'. In *Selected Writings*, ed. Marcus Bullock and Michael Jennings. Translated by Edmund Jephcott, vol. 1, 233–252. Cambridge, MA: Harvard University Press.
Berger, John. 1972. *Ways of Seeing*. London: BBC/Penguin.
Berger, John, and Jean Mohr. [1975] 2010. *A Seventh Man*. London: Verso.
Bhambra, Gurminder. 2009. *Rethinking Modernity: Postcolonialism and the Sociological Imagination*. London: Palgrave Macmillan.
Birnbaum, Antonia. 2016. 'The Obscure Object of Transdisciplinarity. Adorno on the Essay Form'. *Radical Philosophy* July–August. https://www.radicalphilosophy.com/article/the-obscure-object-of-transdisciplinarity.
Bloch, Ernst. 2009. *Heritage of Our Times*. Cambridge: Polity Press.
Braidotti, Rosi, ed. 2013. *After Poststructuralism. Transitions and Transformations*. Vol. 7: *The History of Continental Philosophy*. Durham: Acumen.
Braudel, Fernand. 1995. *The Mediterranean and the Mediterranean World in the Age of Philip II*. Translated by Sian Reynolds. Berkeley: University of California Press.
Brown, Victoria. 2014. *Feminism, Time and Non-Linear History*. New York: Palgrave Macmillan.
Burke, Edmund, III. 1988. 'Islam and Social Movements: Methodological Reflections'. In Edmund Burke, III, and Ira M. Lapidus, *Islam. Politics and Social Movements*. Berkeley, Los Angeles and London: University of California Press.
Burke, Edmund, III. 1993. 'Introduction: Marshall G. S. Hodgson and World History'. In *Rethinking World History. Essays on Europe, Islam, and World History*, ix–xxi. Cambridge: Cambridge University Press.
Butler, Judith. 2004. 'Jews and the Bi-National Vision'. *Logos* 3, no. 1.http://www.logosjournal.com/butler.htm.
Butler, Judith. 2007. 'I Merely Belong to Them'. *London Review of Books* 29, no. 9. http://www.lrb.co.uk/v29/n09/judith-butler/i-merely-belong-to-them.
Butler, Judith. 2012. *Parting Ways: Jewishness and the Critique of Zionism*. New York: Columbia University Press.
Carofalo, Viola. 2013. *Un Pensiero Dannato. Frantz Fanon e la Politica del Riconoscimento*. Milano: Mimesis.
Castoriadis, Cornelius. 2009. *Histoire et Creations. Textes philosophiques inédits (1945–1967)*. Paris: Seuil.
Castro-Gómez, Santiago. 2002. 'The Social Sciences. Epistemic Violence and the Problem of the "Invention of the Other"'. *Nepantla. Views from the South* 3, no. 2: 269–285.
Césaire, Aimé. [1955] 1972. *Discourse on Colonialism*. New York: Monthly Review Press.
Chakrabarty, Dipesh. 1992. 'Postcoloniality and the Artifice of History: Who Speaks for the "Indian" Pasts?'. *Representations* 37: 1–26.
Chakrabarty, Dipesh. 2007. *Provincializing Europe: Postcolonial Thought and Historical Difference*. Princeton: Princeton University Press.
Chakrabarty, Dipesh. 2009. 'The Climate of History: Four Theses'. *Critical Inquiry* 35, no. 2: 197–222.
Chalcraft, John. 2016. *Popular Politics in the Making of the Modern Middle East*. Cambridge: Cambridge University Press.

Chambers, Iain. 2008. *Mediterranean Crossings. The Politics of an Interrupted Modernity.* Durham: Duke University Press.
Chambers, Iain. 2013. 'The "Unseen Order"'. In *The Postcolonial Gramsci*, ed. Neelam Srivastava and Baidik Bhattacharya. London and New York Routledge.
Chambers, Iain, and Lidia Curti, eds. 1996. *The Postcolonial Question. Common skies, divided horizons.* London: Routledge.
Chatterjee, Partha. 2003. 'The Nation in Heterogeneous Time'. In *Grounds of Comparison, Around the Work of Benedict Anderson*, ed. Jonathan Culler and Pheng Cheah. London and New York: Rutledge.
Clifford, James. 2013. *Returns. Becoming Indigenous in the Twenty-First Century.* Cambridge: Harvard University Press.
Comaroff, Jean, and John Comaroff. 2012. *Theory from the South. Or, How Euro-America Is Evolving Towards Africa.* Boulder, CO: Paradigm.
Conelli, Carmine. 2012. 'Per una storia postcoloniale del Mezzogiorno'. MA thesis, University of Naples, L'Orientale.
Connell, Kieran, and Matthew Hilton, eds. 2016. *Cultural Studies 50 Years On.* London and New York: Rowman & Littlefield International.
Connell, Raewyn. 2007. *Southern Theory. Social Science and the Global Dynamics of Knowledge.* London: Polity.
Cooper, Mike. 2009. 'Deportee (Plane Wreck at Los Gatos)'. https://www.youtube.com/watch?v=uWWcQ73j-hE .
Costantini, Dino. 2006. *Una malattia europea.* Pisa: Edizioni Plus.
Curti, Lidia. 2017. 'Il soggetto imprevisto. Sulle tracce di Simone de Beauvoir'. In *Genealogie della modernità. Teoria radicale e critica postcoloniale*, ed. Carmine Conelli and Eleonora Meo. Milan: Mimesisi.
Curtis, Mark. 2016. 'Britain's New African Empire'. *Huffpost Business*, July 26.
Dabashi, Hamid. 2012. *The Arab Spring: The End of Postcolonialism.* London: Zed Books.
Dal Lago, Alessandro. 2009. *Non-Persons: The Exclusion of Migrants in a Global Society.* Translated by Marie Orton. Milan: IPOC.
Danielson, Virginia. 1997. *The Voice of Egypt: Umm Kalthūm, Arabic Song, and Egyptian Society in the Twentieth Century.* Chicago: University of Chicago Press.
Dardot, Pierre. 2013. 'Le capitalisme à la lumière du néolibéralisme'. *Raisons politiques* 52: 13–24.
Dardot, Pierre, and Christian Laval. 2013 *The New Way of the World: On Neoliberal Society.* London: Verso.
Davies, Will. 2014. *The Limits of Neoliberalism: Authority, Sovereignty and the Logic of Competition.* London: Sage.
de Certeau, Michel, 1993. *The Writing of History.* Translated by Tom Conley. New York: Columbia University Press.
De Martino, Ernesto. 1961. *La terra del rimorso. Contributi a una storia religiosa del Sud.* Milan: Il Saggiatore.
D'Eramo, Marco. 2013. 'Populism and the New Oligarchy'. *New Left Review* 82 (July–August): 5–28.
De Smet, Brecht. 2016. *Gramsci on Tahrir. Revolution and Counter-Revolution in Egypt.* London: Pluto Press.
Deleuze, Gilles. 2006. *The Fold.* London and New York: Continuum.
Derrida, Jacques. 1998. *Archive Fever: A Freudian Impression.* Chicago: University of Chicago Press.
Derrida, Jacques. 2000. *Of Hospitality.* Stanford: Stanford University Press.
Diagne, Souleymane Bachir. 2013. 'On the Postcolonial and the Universal?' *Rue Descartes*, no. 78. http://www.ruedescartes.org/articles/2013-2-on-the-postcolonial-and-the-universal/.
Diawara, Manthia. 2001. 'The 1960s in Bamako: Malick Sidibé and James Brown'. http://warholfoundation.org/grant/paper11/paper.html.

Didi-Huberman, Georges. 2000. *Devant le temps. Histories de l'art et anachronisme des images*. Paris: Éditions de Minuit.
Djebar, Assia. 1992. *Women of Algiers in Their Apartments*. Translated by Marjolijn de Jager. Charlottesville: University Press of Virginia.
Durham, Jimmie. 1994. *A Certain Lack of Coherence. Writings on Art and Cultural Politics*. London: Kala Press.
Elhaik, Tarek. 2016. *The Incurable Image*. Edinburgh: Edinburgh University Press 2016.
Eley, Geoff. 2002. 'Politics, Culture, and the Public Sphere'. *Positions* 10, no. 1: 219–236.
Eshun, Kodwu. 2007. "Drawing the Forms of Things Unknown". In *The Ghosts of Songs. The Film Art of the Black Audio Collective*, ed. K. Eshun and A. Sagar. Liverpool: University of Liverpool Press.
Ettinger, Bracha. 2006. *The Matrixial Borderspace*. Minneapolis: University of Minnesota Press.
Fahmy, Khaled. 2015. 'The Long Revolution'. https://aeon.co/essays/how-the-egyptian-revolution-began-and-where-it-might-end .
Fairlie, Simon. 2007. 'A Short History of Enclosure in Britain'. *The Land* 7. http://www.thelandmagazine.org.uk/articles/short-history-enclosure-britain.
Fanon, Frantz. 1986. *Black Skin, White Masks*. Translated by Charles Lam Markmann, with forewords by Ziauddin Sardar and Homi K. Bhabha. London: Pluto Press.
Fanon, Frantz. 2004. *The Wretched of the Earth*. Translated by Richard Philcox, with commentary by Jean-Paul Sartre and Homi K. Bhabha. New York: Grove Press.
Featherstone, David. 2008. *Resistance, Space and Political Identities: The Making of Counter-Global Networks*. Oxford: Wiley-Blackwell.
Federici, Silvia. 2004. *Caliban and the Witch: Women, the Body and Primitive Accumulation*. New York: Autonomedia.
Fischer, Sibylle. 2004. *Modernity Disavowed: Haiti and the Cultures of Slavery in the Age of Revolution*. Durham: Duke University Press.
Foucault, Michel. 1972. *The Archaeology of Knowledge and the Discourse on Language*. Translated by A.M. Sheridan Smith. New York: Pantheon Books.
Foucault, Michel. 1986. 'Of Other Spaces'. Translated by J. Miskowiec. *Diacritics* 16, no. 1: 22–27.
Foucault, Michel. 2004. *Society Must Be Defended, Lectures at the Collège de France, 1975–76* . Translated by David Macey. London: Penguin.
Gérardot, Maie. 2007. 'Penser en rythmes. Pistes de réflexion pour la géographie'. Espaces-Temps.net . http://www.espacestemps.net/articles/penser-en-rythmes/.
Ghosh, Amitav. 1994. *In an Antique Land*. New York: Vintage Books, 1994.
Gilroy, Paul. 1993. *The Black Atlantic. Modernity and Double Consciousness*. London: Verso.
Gilroy, Paul. 2004. *After Empire. Melancholia or Convivial Culture?* London and New York: Routledge.
Giroux, Henry. 2004. 'Public Pedagogy and the Politics of Neoliberalism: Making the Political More Pedagogical'. *Policy Futures in Education* 2, no. 4: 494–503.
Goitein, S.D. 1999. *A Mediterranean Society* (An Abridgment in One Volume). Revised and edited by Jacob Lassner. Berkeley: University of California Press.
Goodman, Steve. 2010. *Sonic Warfare: Sound, Affect and the Ecology of Fear*. Cambridge: MIT Press.
Gramsci, Antonio. 1975. *Quaderni del Carcere*. Turin: Einaudi.
Gramsci, Antonio. 2015. *The Southern Question*. New York: Bordighera Press.
Gregory, Derek. 2004. *The Colonial Present*. Oxford: Blackwell.
Guha, Ranajit. 2004. *History at the Limit of World-History*. New York: Columbia University Press.
Guhin, Jeffrey, and Jonathan Wyrtzen. 2013. 'The Violences of Knowledge: Edward Said, Sociology and Post-Orientalist Reflexivity'. In *Postcolonial Sociology (Political Power and Social Theory*, ed. Julian Go, vol. 24, 231–262.
Habermas, Jürgen. 1992. *The Structural Transformation of the Public Sphere: Inquiry into a Category of Bourgeois Society*. Oxford: Polity Press.

Bibliography

Hall, Catherine, Keith McClelland, Nick Draper, Kate Donington, and Rachel Lang. 2014. *Legacies of British Slave-Ownership: Colonial Slavery and the Formation of Victorian Britain*. Cambridge: Cambridge University Press.

Hall, Stuart. 1988. 'New Ethnicities'. In *Black Film, British Cinema*, ed. Koben Mercer. London: BFI/ICA Documents 7.

Hall, Stuart. 1996. 'Thinking at the Limit. When Was the Postcolonial?' In *The Postcolonial Question. Common skies, Divided Horizons*, ed. Iain Chambers and Lidia Curti. London: Routledge.

Hall, Stuart, Chas Critcher, Tony Jefferson, John Clarke, and Brian Roberts. [1978] 2013. *Policing the Crisis: Mugging, the State and Law and Order*. London: Palgrave Macmillan.

Hallaq, Wael. 2013 *The Impossible State. Islam, Politics, and Modernity's Moral Predicament*. New York: Columbia University Press.

Hallaq, Wael. 2014, 'Knowledge as Politics by Other Means. An Interview with Wael Hallaq'. *Jadaliyya*. http://www.jadaliyya.com/pages/index/17677/knowledge-as-politics-by-other-means_an-interview.

Hamilakis, Yannis. 2011. 'Indigenous Archaeologies in Ottoman Greece'. In *Scramble for the Past: A Story of Archaeology in the Ottoman Empire 1753–1914*, ed. Z. Bahrani, Z. Celik, and E. Eldem. Istanbul: Salt.

Hardt, Michael, and Sandro Mezzadra. 2015. 'Capitalist Operations: Extraction, Finance, Logistics & Infrastructure'. Pt. 1. https://www.youtube.com/watch?v=zoGv-7jPxoA.

Harney, Stefano, and Fred Moten. 2013. *The Undercommons, Fugitive Planning and Black Study*. New York: Autonomedia.

Hassan, Salah, and Olu Oguibe, eds. 2002. *Authentic/Ex-centric: Conceptualism in Contemporary African Art*. London: Art Data.

Hauser, Gerard. 1999. *Vernacular Voices: The Rhetorics of Publics and Private Spheres*. Columbia: University of South Carolina.

Hay, Douglas, et al. 2011. *Albion's Fatal Tree: Crime and Society in Eighteenth-Century England*. London: Verso.

Hickle, Jason. 2015. 'Enough of Aid—Let's Talk Reparation'. *Guardian*, November 27.

Henriques, Julian. 2011. *Sonic Bodies: Reggae Sound Systems, Performance Techniques, and Ways of Knowing*. London: Continuum.

Hodgkinson, Tim. 2016. *Music and the Myth of Wholeness: Towards a New Aesthetic Paradigm*. Cambridge: MIT Press.

Hodgson, Marshall G.S. 1977. *The Venture of Islam*. 3 vols. Chicago: University of Chicago Press.

Hodgson, Marshall G.S. 2010. *Rethinking World History. Essays on Europe, Islam, and World History*. Cambridge: Cambridge University Press, 2010.

Holston, James, and Arjun Appadurai. 1996. 'Cities and Citizenship'. *Public Culture* 8, no. 2: 187–204.

Hossfeld, Johannes, ed. 2017. *Ten Cities*. Leipzig: Spector Books.

Hussein, Ali Agrama. 2012. *Questioning Secularism: Islam, Sovereignty, and the Rule of Law in Modern Egypt*. Chicago: University of Chicago Press.

Iuliano, Fiorenzo. 2012. *Altri mondi, altre parole. Gayatri Chakravorty Spivak tra decostruzione e impegno militante*. Verona: Ombre Corte.

James, C.L.R. 1989. *The Black Jacobins: Touissant L'Ouverture and the San Domingo Revolution*. New York: Vintage Books.

James, C.L.R. 1994. *Beyond a Boundary*. London: Serpent's Tail.

Jensen, Steven L.B. 2016. 'Decolonization—Not Western Liberals—Established Human Rights on the Global Agenda'. *Open Democracy*, September 29.

Johnson, Linton Kwesi. 1975. *Dread Beat and Blood*. London: Bogle-L'Ouverture.

Kelley, Robin D.G. 1994. *Race Rebels: Culture, Politics, and the Black Working Class*. New York: Free Press.

Khaldûn, Ibn. 2005. *The Muqaddimah. An Introduction to History*. Princeton: Princeton University Press.

Koselleck, Reinhart. 2004. *Futures Past. On the Semantics of Historical Time*. New York: Columbia University Press.

Koselleck, Reinhart. 2007. *Futuro Passato. Per una semantica dei tempi storici*. Bologna: Clueb.
Kureishi, Hanif. 2005. *Word and the Bomb*. London: Faber & Faber.
Le Goff, Jacques. 1992. *History and Memory*. New York: Columbia University Press.
Lemke, Thomas. 2001. '"The Birth of Biopolitics": Michel Foucault's Lecture at the Collège de France on Neoliberal Governmentality'. *Economy and Society* 30, no. 2: 190–207.
Léothaud, Gilles, and Bernard Lortat-Jacob. 2000. 'La Voix méditerranéenne. Une identité problématique'. In *La Vocalité dans les pays d'Europe méridionale et dans le bassin méditerranéen*, ed. Luc Charles-Dominique and Jérôme Cler. Saint-Jouin-de-Milly: Modal Éditions.
Linebaugh, Peter, and Marcus Rediker. 2002. *The Many-Headed Hydra. Sailors, Slaves, Commoners, and the Hidden History of the Revolutionary Atlantic*. Boston: Beacon Press.
Liu, Lydia H. 2014. 'The Eventfulness of Translation: Temporality, Difference, and Competing Universals'. *Translation* 4: 147–170.
Lonzi, Carla. 2010. *Autoritratto*. Milan: et al., 2010.
Losurdo, Domenico. 2014. *Liberalism. A Counter-History*. London: Verso.
Lowe, Lisa. 2015. *The Intimacies of Four Continents*. Durham: Duke University Press.
Lusini, Valentina. 2013. *Destinazione mondo. Forme e politiche dell'alterità nell'arte contemporanea*. Verona: Ombre Corte.
MacDonald, Sharon. 2008. *Difficult Heritage: Negotiating the Nazi Past in Nuremberg and Beyond*. London and New York: Routledge.
Madley, Benjamin. 2015. 'Reexamining the American Genocide Debate: Meaning, Historiography, and New Methods'. *American Historical Review* 120, no. 1: 98–139.
Magdy, Rana 2014. 'Cairo: A History of People's Rights to the City'. http://www.opendemocracy.net/arab-awakening/rana-nessim/cairo-history-of-people's-right-to-city.
Makdisi, George. 1990. *The Rise of Humanism in Classical Islam and the Christian West: With Special Reference to Scholasticism*. Edinburgh: Edinburgh University Press.
Mammone, Andrea, Ercole Giap Parini, and Giuseppe A. Veltri, eds. 2015. *The Routledge Handbook of Contemporary Italy*. London: Routledge.
Mamdani, Mahmood. 2013. 'Reading Ibn Khaldun in Kampala'. http://criticalencounters.net/2013/07/05/reading-ibn-khaldun-in-kampala-mahmood-mamdani/.
Marcus, George, and Fred Myers, eds. 1995. *The Traffic in Culture. Refiguring Art and Anthropology*. Berkeley: University of California Press.
Marino, Alessandra. 2015. *Acts of Angry Writing: On Citizenship and Orientalism in Postcolonial India*. Detroit: Wayne State University Press.
Mazower, Mark. 2005. *Salonica. City of Ghosts. Christians, Muslims and Jews 1430–1950*. London: HarperPerennial.
Mbembe, Achille. 2001. *On the Postcolony*. Berkeley: University of California Press.
Mbembe, Achille. 2009. 'What Is Postcolonial Thinking? An Interview with Achille Mbembe'. *Eurozine*. www.eurozine.com/articles/2008-01-09-mbembe-en.html.
Mbembe, Achille. 2013a. *Sortir de la Grande Nuit*. Paris: La Découverte.
Mbembe, Achille. 2013b. 'Africa Theorizes. Tony Bogues and Achille Mbembe'. https://www.youtube.com/watch?v=brvLjfhslCg.
Mellino, Miguel. 2013. *Cittadinanza postcoloniali, Appartenze, razze e razzismo in Europa e in Italia*. Rome: Carocci.
Mezzadra, Sandro. 2006. *Diritto di fuga, migranti, cittadinanza, globalizzazione*. Verona: ombre corte.
Mezzadra, Sandro. 2011. 'Bringing Capital Back In: A Materialist Turn in Postcolonial Studies?' *Inter-Asian Cultural Studies* 12, no. 1: 154–164.
Mezzadra, Sandro, and Brett Neilson. 2013. *Border as Method, or, the Multiplication of Labor*. Durham: Duke University Press.
Mezzadra, Sandro, and Federico Rahola. 2006. 'The Postcolonial Condition: A Few Notes on the Quality of Historical Time in the Global Present'. *Postcolonial Text* 2, no. 1. http://postcolonial.org/index.php/pct/article/view/393/819.

Mignolo, Walter D. 2010. 'Delinking. The Rhetoric of Modernity, the Logic of Coloniality and the Grammar of De-coloniality'. In *Globalisation and the Decolonial Option*, ed. Mignolo and Escobar. London: Routledge.
Mignolo, Walter D. 2015. 'Geopolitics of Sensing and Knowing: On (De)Coloniality, Border Thinking, and Epistemic Disobedience'. *eipcp*. http://eipcp.net/transversal/0112/mignolo/en.
Mignolo, Walter D., and Arturo Escobar, eds. 2010. *Globalisation and the Decolonial Option*. London: Routledge.
Mohanty, Chandra Talpade. 2003. *Feminism Without Borders. Decolonizing Theory, Practicing Solidarity*. Durham: Duke University Press.
Morana, Mabel, and Enrique Dessel, eds. 2008. *Coloniality at Large: Latin America and the Postcolonial Debate*. Durham: Duke University Press.
Moten, Fred. 2003. *In the Break: The Aesthetics of the Black Radical Tradition*. Minneapolis: University of Minnesota Press.
Mouffe, Chantal. 2000. *The Democratic Paradox*. London: Verso.
Mutman, Mahmut. 2014. *The Politics of Writing Islam: Voicing Difference*. London: Bloomsbury.
Nietzsche, Friedrich. 1997. 'On the Use and Abuse of History for Life'. In *Untimely Meditations*. Translated by R.J. Hollingdale. Cambridge: Cambridge University Press.
Oberoi, Pia. 2015. 'What's in a Name? The Complex Reality of Migration and Human Rights in the Twenty-First Century'. *Open Democracy*, October 15.
Oguibe, Olu. 2005. 'The True Location of Ernest Mancoba's Modernism'. *Third Text* 19, no. 4: 419–426.
Oliver, Paul. 2001. *Savannah Syncopators. African Retentions in the Blues*. London: Studio Vista.
Palladino, Mariangela, and John Miller, eds. 2015. *The Globalization of Space*. London: Pickering & Chatto.
Pappé, Ilan, ed. 2015. *Israel and South Africa: The Many Faces of Apartheid*. London: Zed Books.
Park, Peter K.J. 2013. *Africa, Asia, and the History of Philosophy. Racism and the Formation of the Philosophical Canon, 1780–1830*. Albany: States University of New York Press.
Parvan, Oana. 2014. 'Beyond the "Arab Spring": New Media, Art and Counter-Information in post-revolutionary North Africa'. *Anglistica*. http://www.anglistica-aion-unior.org.
Perugini, Nicola, and Neve Gordon. 2015. *The Human Right to Dominate*. New York: Oxford University Press.
Perugini, Nicola, and Francesco Zucconi. 2012. 'False Syllogisms, Troublesome Combinations and Primo Levi's Political Positioning on Israel and Palestine'. https://www.opendemocracy.net/nicola-perugini-francesco-zucconi/false-syllogisms-troublesome-combinations-and-primo-levi's-politic.
Peters, Michael A., and Ergin Bulut, eds. 2011. *Cognitive Capitalism, Education and Digital Labor*. Bern: Peter Lang.
Piketty, Thomas. 2014. *Capital in the Twenty-First Century*. Cambridge: Harvard University Press.
Poulantzas, Nicos. 1973. *Political Power and Social Classes*. London: New Left Books.
Quijano, Anibal. 2000. 'Coloniality of Power, Eurocentrism, and Latin America'. *Nepentla: Views from the South* 1, no. 3: 533–580.
Rabinow, Paul. 2007. *Marking Time: On the Anthropology of the Contemporary*. Princeton: University of Princeton Press.
Racy, A.J. 2004. *Making Music in the Arab World: The Culture and Artistry of Tarab*. Cambridge: Cambridge University Press.
Renault, Matthieu. 2013. 'Fanon e la decolonizzazione del sapere. Teorie in viaggio nella situazione (post)coloniale'. In *Fanon postcoloniale. I dannati della terra oggi*, ed. Miguel Mellino. Verona: ombre corte.
Revel, Judith. 2010. *Foucault, une pensée du discontinu*. Paris: Fayard.
Ricœur, Paul. 2006. *Memory, History, Forgetting*. Chicago: University of Chicago Press.
Rodinson, Maxime. 1973. *Israel: A Colonial-Settler State?* New York: Monad Press.

Rosenthal, Mark. ed. 2009. *William Kentridge: Five Themes*. San Francisco: SFMOMA.
Roy, Arundhati. 2014. *Capitalism. A Ghost Story*. London and New York: Verso.
Said, Edward. 1992. *Musical Elaborations*. New York: Vintage Books.
Said, Edward. 1994. *Culture and Imperialism*. New York: Vintage.
Said, Edward. 1997. *Covering Islam. How the Media and the Experts Determine How We See the Rest of the World*. New York: Vintage Books.
Sakai, Naoki. 2011. 'Theory and the West. On the Question of Humanitas and Anthropos'. *Transeuropeennes*. http://www.transeuropeennes.eu/en/articles/316/theory_and_the_west.
Saldanha, Arun. 2007. *Psychedelic White: Goa Trance and the Viscosity of Race*. Minneapolis: University of Minnesota Press.
Salvatore, Armando. 2011. 'Eccentric Modernity? An Islamic Perspective on the Civilizing Process and the Public Sphere'. *European Journal of Social Theory* 14, no. 1: 55–69.
Santos, Boaventura de Sousa. 2007. 'Beyond Abyssal Thinking. From Global Lines to Ecologies of Knowledge'. http://www.eurozine.com/articles/2007-06-29-santos-en.html.
Santos, Boaventura de Sousa. 2014. *Epistemologies of the South. Justice Against Epistemicide*. Boulder, CO: Paradigm.
Sanyal, Kalyan. 2007. *Rethinking Capitalist Development: Primitive Accumulation, Governmentality and Post-Colonial Capitalism*. New Delhi: Routledge.
Schmitt, Carl. 2006. *The Nomos of the Earth in the International Law of the Jus Publicum Europaeum*. Translated by G.L. Ulman. New York: Telos Press Publishing.
Schmitt, Carl. 2015. *Imperium. Conversazioni con Klaus Figge e Dieter Grog 1971*. Translated by Corrado Badocco. Macerata: Quodlibet.
Schneider, Arnd, and Chris Wright. 2010. *Between Art and Anthropology: Contemporary Ethnographic Practice*. Oxford and New York: Berg.
Scott, David. 2004. *Conscripts of Modernity: The Tragedy of Colonial Enlightenment*. Durham: Duke University Press.
Scott, David. 2005. 'The Social Construction of Postcolonial Studies'. In *Postcolonial Studies and Beyond*, ed. Ania Loomba, Suvir Kaul, Matti Bunzi, Antoinette Burton, and Jed Esty. Durham: Duke University Press.
Seikaly, Sherene. 2014. 'Palestine as Archive'. *Jadaliyya*. http://www.jadaliyya.com/pages/index/18760/palestine-as-archive.
Selden, Daniel L. 2014. '"Our Films, Their Films": Postcolonial Critique of the Cinematic Apparatus'. *Postcolonial Studies* 17, no. 4: 382–414.
Shamma, Naseer. 2003. *Maqamat Ziryáb: Desde el Eúfrates al Guadalaquivir*. CD. Madrid: Pneuma.
Shohat, Ella. 1992. 'Notes on the "Post-Colonial"'. *Social Text* 31/32: 99–113.
Smith, Linda Tuhiwai. 2012. *Decolonizing Methodologies. Research and Indigenous Peoples*. London: Zed Books.
Spivak, Gayatri Charkravorty. 1988. 'Can the Subaltern Speak?' In *Marxism and the Interpretation of Culture*, ed. Cary Nelson and Lawrence Grossberg. Champaign: University of Illinois Press.
Spivak, Gayatri Chakravorty. 1999. *A Critique of Postcolonial Reason: Toward a History of the Vanishing Present*. Cambridge: Harvard University Press.
Stacey, Jackie. 2016. 'Idealizations and Their Discontents: Feminism and the Field Imaginary of Cultural Studies'. In *Cultural Studies 50 years on*, ed. Kieran Connell and Matthew Hilton. London and New York: Rowman & Littlefield International.
Stoler, Ann Laura. 2009. *Along the Archival Grain. Epistemic Anxieties and Colonial Common Sense*. Princeton: Princeton University Press.
Stoler, Ann Laura, Martina Tazzioli, and Oliver Belcher. 2015. 'Interview with Ann Laura Stoler'. *darkmatter—in the ruins of imperial culture*. http://www.darkmatter101.org/site/2015/10/05/interview-with-ann-laura-stoler/.
Swanton, Daniel. 2008. 'The Force of Race'. *darkmatter—in the ruins of imperial culture*. http://www.darkmatter101.org/site/2008/02/23/the-force-of-race/.
Tazzioli, Martina. 2015. *Spaces of Governmentality: Autonomous Migrations and the Arab Uprisings*. London and New York: Rowman & Littlefield.

Taussig, Michael. 1991. *Shamanism, Colonialism, and the Wild Man. A Study in Terror and Healing*. Chicago: University of Chicago Press.
Tawadros, Gilane, and Sarah Campbell, eds. 2003. *Fault Lines: Contemporary African Art and Shifting Landscapes*. London: InIVA.
Terranova, Tiziana. 2009. 'Another Life. The Nature of Political Economy in Foucault's Genealogy of Biopolitics'. *Theory, Culture & Society* 26, no. 6: 234–262.
Thompson, E.P. 2013. *Whigs and Hunters. The Origin of the Black Act*. London: Breviary Stuff.
Todorov, Tzevtan. 1992. *The Conquest of America. The Question of the Other*. New York: HarperPerennial.
Tognonato, Claudio. 2014. 'In Argentina un golpe di mercato'. *il manifesto*, January 27.
Trouillot, Michel-Rolph.1995. *Silencing the Past. Power and the Production of History*. Boston: Beacon Press.
Vattimo, Gianni.1988. 'Bottles, Nets, Revolution, and the Tasks of Philosophy'. *Cultural Studies* 2, no. 2: 143–151.
Walcott, Derek. 1992. 'The Schooner "Flight"'. In *Collected Poems*. London: Faber & Faber.
Watson, Mark. 2015. '"Centring the Indigenous'. Postcommodity's Trans-Indigenous Relational Art"'. *Third Text* 29, no. 3: 141–154.
Weizman, Eyal. 2007. *Hollow Land: Israel's Architecture of Occupation*. London: Verso.
Weizman, Eyal. 2009. 'Lawfare in Gaza: Legislative Attack'. http://www.opendemocracy.net/article/legislative-attack.
Wilson, Ivy G. 2011. *Specters of Democracy*. Oxford: Oxford University Press.
Wolfe, Patrick. 2006. 'Settler Colonialism and the Elimination of the Native'. *Journal of Genocide Research* 8, no. 4: 387–409.
Yimer, Dagmawi. 2015. *Asmat—Nomi per tutte le vittime in mare*. https://vimeo.com/114849871.
Young, Robert. 1990. *White Mythologies: Writing History and the West*. London: Routledge.
Zaatari, Akram. 2013. *Time Capsule*. Seminar held at the University of Naples, L'Orientale, December 16–18.
Zapperi, Giovanna, 2015. 'Il tempo del femminismo. Soggettività e storia in Carla Lonzi'. *Studi Culturali* 1: 63–82.
Zielinski, Siegfried, and Franziska Latell. 2010. 'How One Sees'. In *Variantology 4. On Deep Time Relations of Arts, Sciences and Technologies in the Arabic-Islamic World and Beyond*, ed. Siegfried Zielinski and Eckhardt Fürlus. Cologne: Walter König.

Index

Abu l-Hasan 'Ali Ibn Nafi (Zíryáb), 95
Abu Lughod, Janet, 122
Aboriginal dot paintings, 93
Abulafia, David, 121; *The Great Sea: A Human History of the Mediterranean*, 121
Abu Qir Bay (Battle of the Nile), 109, 122
Aden, 123
Adorno, Theodor.W., 8, 13
Afghanistan, 67, 68, 126
Africa, 9, 20, 21, 25, 51, 53, 62, 63, 64, 71, 75, 83, 86, 106, 109, 117, 124, 126; colonial, 5, 12, 24, 28, 49; modernity of, 95–99; regime change, 65–68
Agamben, Giorgio, 39, 40
Akomfrah, John, 90; *The Nine Muses*, 90
Alessandrini, Anthony, 66
Algeria, 28, 47–48, 76, 119
Algiers, 86
Alioua, Mehdi, 75
Al Jazeera, 68
Althusser, Louis, 7
Americas, 28, 49, 83, 86
Appaduria, Arjun, 34
Arab Spring, 27, 63–67; neoliberalism, 28, 68; revolutionary character, 18, 63–65, 66, 67, 69
Araeen, Rasheed, 98
archive, 4, 6, 6–7, 11, 14, 34, 48, 52, 71, 79, 84, 86–87, 88, 89, 91, 96, 97, 98, 100n27, 101–102, 107, 108, 110, 117–119, 121–122, 123, 125, 126; colonial, 9, 19, 27, 31–34, 38, 49, 95, 109; maritime, 109–110; music as, 111–114; landscape as, 85
Arendt, Hannah, 38, 49, 77, 87
Argentina, 54
art, 11–12, 32, 56–57, 84, 86, 88, 90, 91–95, 97–99, 111, 113; anthropology, 59, 93; postcolonial, 58, 59, 92, 95. *See also* Africa, modernity of
Asia, 28, 49, 75, 86, 106, 117
Ascione, Gennaro, 23
Atris, Abu, 68
Australia, 75, 105, 106

Baez, Joan, 83
Baghdad, 122
Baldwin, James, 19, 23, 29, 48, 58, 61
Balibar, Étienne, 38, 72
Beckett, Samuel, 90
belonging, 14, 33, 38, 44, 54, 71–72, 74–75, 78, 85, 90, 105, 110, 112, 117, 123; citizenship, 108; European, 27; musical, 62
Belting, Hans, 21
Ben M'Hidi, Larbi, 47
Benjamin, Walter, 22, 31, 77, 101, 111, 115, 121; *Theses on the Philosophy of History*, 115
Berger, John, 1
Berlin, 61, 62, 63, 88, 93

Bernal, Martin, 117; *Black Athena*, 117
Bhabha, Homi, 71
Bhambra, Gurminder, 116; *Rethinking Modernity*, 116
bio-politics, 38, 70, 78, 105–106
Birnbaum, Antonia, 13
Black Panthers, 29, 48
body, 12, 38, 51–52, 58, 62, 90, 107, 113, 120; migrant, 51, 84; postcolonial, 46, 126
borders, 39, 44, 55, 71, 72, 77, 94, 103, 104–106, 108, 117; disciplinary, 12, 23
Braithwaite, Edward Kamau, 107
Braudel, Ferdinand, 117, 121
Bristol, 62, 63
British Empire, 28, 97, 109
Brown, James, 99
Browne, Victoria, 24
Buenos Aires, 51
Butler, Judith, 49, 77

Cairo, 51, 62, 122
Canada, 105
capitalism, 4, 14, 27, 29, 40, 43, 54, 57, 65, 74, 98, 103–104
Caribbean, 76, 90, 107, 109
Castel Volturno, 83
Castro-Gómez, Santiago, 22
Césaire, Aimé, 8, 47, 48–49
Chatterjee, Partha, 101, 106
China, 43
Chile, 51
Chrakrabarty, Dipesh, 21, 31, 54, 61, 108; *Provincializing Europe: Postcolonial Thought and Historical Difference*, 31
Christianity, 20, 33, 70, 80, 121, 123
citizenship, 2, 5, 8, 9, 13, 22, 38, 57, 62–63, 72–73, 76–77, 87, 90, 105, 108, 126
Clifford, James, 55
Coleridge, Samuel Taylor, 90; *The Rime of the Ancient Mariner*, 90
colonialism, 4, 5, 9, 13, 18, 20, 22, 29, 32–33, 39, 42, 46, 47–49, 57–58, 72, 89, 98, 99, 119, 122; capitalism, 4, 14, 18, 29, 37, 103; democracy, 76; race, 27; totalitarianism, 52. *See also* Europe
Comoroff, Jean, 96
Comoroff, John, 96

Condée, Maysée, 107
Congo, 57
Conrad, Joseph, 27, 33
Constantinople, 123
Cooper, Mike,, 83, 84
Corriere della Sera , 65
Cuba, 109

Dal Lago, Alessandro, 75
Damascus, 122
Dardot, Pierre, 40, 54
de Certeau, Michel, 34
Deleuze, Gilles, 56, 103, 112
De Martino, Ernesto, 44
democracy, 1, 2–3, 5, 8, 13, 19, 20, 22, 26, 29, 38, 40, 42, 45, 53, 55, 57, 62–63, 64, 66, 68, 70–73, 74, 74–76, 109
Derrida, Jacques, 74, 97, 121
Diagne, Souleymane Bachir, 57
Dider-Huberman, Georges, 90
Djebar, Assia, 74
Durham, Jimmie, 92–94
Dussel, Enrique, 21

Egypt, 28, 65, 66–69, 109, 117, 122, 124
Eichmann, Adolf, 77
Elhaik, Tarek, 6
Eliot, T.S., 90
El Paso, 106
Enlightenment, 8, 23, 70, 73, 108
Etchevehere, Miguel, 53
Ethiopia, 117
ethnicity, 12, 45–46, 54, 93
Ettinger, Bracha, 111
Europe, 17, 19, 20–22, 23, 25, 27–28, 31, 34, 37, 43, 45, 47, 49, 54, 57, 61, 64, 68, 70, 75, 80, 86, 89, 91, 92, 94, 97, 98, 106, 109–110, 111, 113, 115–116, 117, 119, 121, 122, 123–124

Fanon, Frantz, 12, 23, 29, 33, 45, 46, 47, 48, 50, 55, 57, 58, 70, 74, 80, 91; *The Wretched of the Earth*, 45
Federici, Silvia, 43
Fischer, Sibylle, 77–78
France, 28, 64, 119
Freeman, Elizabeth, 64
Freud, Sigmund, 110, 121, 123

Friedrich, Caspar David, 90; *The Wanderer above the Mists*, 90
Front de Libération Nationale [FLN], 47
Foucault, Michel, 25, 27, 52, 65, 70, 78, 91, 101, 102–104, 107, 121; *The Archaeology of Knowledge*, 27; *The Order of Things*, 103
Frontex, 75
Fustat (Cairo), 122, 123

Gaza, 34, 48, 77
Geniza (Fustat), 123
genocide, 4, 5, 20, 41, 49, 58, 63, 73, 89, 104
geography, 20, 22, 26, 28, 48, 54, 61, 91, 102, 110, 119, 121
Ghosh, Amitav, 30
Gilroy, Paul, 57, 72, 83
Glissant, Edouard, 107
Goitein, Shalom Dov, 21, 122–123; *A Mediterranean Society*, 21
Goodman, Steve, 111
governmentality, 52
Gramsci, Antonio, 7, 32, 44, 54, 55, 61, 112, 121; *Prison Notebooks*, 8
Greece, 28, 117
Greeks, 45
Gregory, Derek, 119
Guattari, Félix, 56, 112
Guha, Ranjit, 22, 47, 110, 115; *History at the Limit of World-History*, 47
Guthrie, Woody, 83

Habermas, Jürgen, 62, 77
Haiti, 28, 48, 65, 109, 116
Hall, Stuart, 18, 45, 48, 120
Hamas, 48
Hamilakis, Yannis, 117
Haneke, Michael, 119; *Caché* (2005), 119
Hegel, Georg Wilhelm Friedrich, 22, 95, 110, 115, 116
Heidegger, Martin, 17, 103
Hellenism, 117
Henriques, Julien, 114
heterotopia, 44, 101, 102–104, 107
history, 1, 2, 3, 5, 6, 8–9, 11–12, 13, 14, 18, 19, 21, 24, 27, 29, 31, 33, 34, 39–40, 42–43, 46–50, 55, 56, 57, 58–59, 62, 64–65, 72, 74, 79, 80, 84–85, 86, 87, 88, 89, 90–91, 93, 94, 95, 96–99, 101, 103, 104, 109–116, 117, 119–124, 126; connected, 116; historicism, 3, 8, 18, 20, 24, 31, 91, 92, 95, 110, 121; failure of, 27, 95. *See also* archive; knowledge; memory
Hobbes, Thomas, 40
Hodgson, Marshall, 124; *The Venture of Islam*, 124
Holocaust, 49
Homeland Security, 75
Horkheimer, Max, 8
Horn of Africa, 68
humanism, 19, 21, 24, 29, 39, 41, 45, 46–47, 57–58, 70, 76, 87, 103, 116

Ibn al-Haythan (Alhazen), 21
Ibn Khaldûn:, 21, 62; *The Muqaddimah. An Introduction to History*, 21
India, 29, 76, 90
International Monetary Fund, 51, 64, 98
Iranian revolution, 65
Iraq, 67
Ireland, 28, 29, 30
Islam, 20, 21, 33, 65, 67, 70, 118, 121, 123–124
Israel, 49, 57, 104
Italy, 28, 61

James, C.L.R., 41, 48, 69; *Beyond a Boundary*, 69; *The Black Jacobins: Touissant L'Ouverture and the San Domingo Revolution*, 41, 69
Johannesburg, 53, 62
Juarez, 106
Judaism, 20, 121, 123
Julien, Isaac, 83; *Western Union, Small Boats*, 83

Kalthūm, Umm, 112–113
Kant, Immanuel, 50; *A Critique of Postcolonial Reason*, 50
Keifer, Anselm, 93
Kentridge, William, 15
Kenya, 63
Kiev, 62, 123
Koselleck, Reinhart, 31, 32
knowledge, 1, 2, 3–4, 6–10, 12–14, 15n18, 19, 22–26, 29, 33, 37, 39, 55, 57, 62,

71, 72, 73, 84, 87, 88–89, 91, 95, 103, 115, 115–117, 118, 119, 121, 125, 127; colonialism, 7, 13; economy, 106–107; presumed neutrality, 6, 7, 8, 12, 23, 25, 72, 74, 78, 86, 93, 106, 111, 122
Kuhn, T. S., 25
Kurdistan, 106
Kureishi, Hanif, 5

Lagos, 62, 99
Lampedusa, 33, 83, 86–87, 125
Latin America, 29, 75, 86, 126
Lefebvre, Henri, 103

Le Goff, Jacques, 85

Lemke, Thomas, 52
Laval, Christian, 40
Léothaud, Gilles, 113
Levi, Carlo, 44; *Christ stopped at Eboli*, 44
Levi, Primo, 49
Lévinas, Emmanuel, 46
liberalism, 7, 21, 27, 29, 40–42, 52–53, 58, 68, 73, 74, 75. *See also* neoliberalism
Libya, 5, 67
Linebaugh, Peter, 43; *The Many Headed Hydra. Sailors, Slaves, Commoners, and the Hidden History of the Revolutionary Atlantic*, 43
Lisbon, 62
Locke, John, 40, 41, 43
London, 51, 53, 61, 67, 88, 99, 106, 122
Lonzi, Carla, 95
Lortat-Jacob, Bernard, 113
L'Ouverture, Touissant, 48
Los Angeles, 61, 99, 106
Los Gatos, 83
Lowe, Lisa, 21
Luanda, 62, 99

Madrid, 51
Makadisi, George, 21
Malcolm X, 48
Mali, 67, 99
Marcus, George, 59
maritime criticism, 107–110
Marker, Chris, 110; *Sans Soleil*, 110
MatriArchive of the Mediterranean, 100n27

Marley, Bob, 107
Marrakech, 122
Marseilles, 123
Marx, Karl, 43, 54
Mazower, Mark, 123; *Salonica.City of Ghosts. Christians, Muslims and Jews 1430–1950*, 123
Mbembe, Achille, 23
Mediterranean, 1, 21, 33, 45, 47, 55, 61, 64, 66–68, 70–71, 74, 77, 83, 86–87, 100n27, 105–106, 109–110, 111–113, 117–119, 120, 120–124, 125. *See also* archive; migration; music
Memmi, Albert, 49
memory, 11, 13, 33–34, 59, 84–87, 89, 91, 93, 95, 114, 118–119, 121, 123, 126. *See also* archive; history; music
Merleau-Ponty, Maurice, 57
Mezzadra, Sandro, 22, 31, 54, 104
Mignolo, Walter, 21, 22
Migrant Memories Archives (Rome), 125
migration, 1–2, 4, 28, 38–39, 75, 83–84, 86, 88, 90–91, 108, 110; law and, 9, 77; museum of, 87
Milan, 61
Milton, John, 90
Mohr, Jean, 1
Morocco, 123
Mouffe, Chantal, 53
Mubarak, Hosni, 66
Mudimbe, Valentin Y, 49
music, 29, 62, 70–71, 80n6, 84, 88, 96, 111–114, 117; Africa, 80n5; reasoning with, 9, 11, 56, 111, 113–114. *See also* archive; memory
Myers, Fred, 59

Nairobi, 62
Naples, 62, 63, 93, 109, 122
Napoleon, 109
Narbonne, 123
Neapolitan Republic, 109
necropolitics, 24, 87
Neilson, Brett, 22, 54, 104
Nelson, Horatio, 109, 122
neoliberalism, 2, 8, 28, 40, 51, 52, 67–68. *See also* liberalism
New York, 61, 88
New Zealand, 105

Nietzsche, Friedrich, 118, 121

Oceania, 49
Ottoman Empire, 117, 123

Palermo, 83
Palestine, 29, 33–34, 48, 49, 57, 67, 104, 106, 117
Pappé, Ilan, 105
Paris, 61, 65, 88, 106, 119, 122
Pasolini, Pier Paolo, 44
Persia, 124
Perry, Lee 'Scratch', 107
Peru, 117
Piketty, Thomas, 53
Pisa, 123
'Plane Wreck at Los Gatos (Deportee)', 83
Poe, Edgar Allan, 90; *The Narrative of Arthur Gordon Pym*, 90
Pontecorvo, Gillo, 47; *The Battle of Algiers*, 47
Poulantzas, Nicos, 20
philosophy, 15, 21, 23, 62, 76;
    postcolonial, 45–50
Putney Debates, 30

Quetta, 106
Quijano, Anibal, 6

Rahola, Federico, 31
racism, 1–2, 4, 12, 24, 41–42, 70, 73, 74–77, 79–80
Racy, A.J., 114
reason, 13, 19, 21, 22–23, 28–29, 33, 47, 48–50, 64, 76, 96, 108, 115; rationality and, 6, 13, 19, 26, 52, 70, 95, 114; rhythm and, 24, 84–85, 113, 120
Rediker, Marcus, 43; *The Many Headed Hydra. Sailors, Slaves, Commoners, and the Hidden History of the Revolutionary Atlantic*, 43
Renaissance, 17, 124
Renault, Matthieu, 33
Ricœur, Paul, 84, 90
rights, 5, 9, 20, 26, 28, 29–30, 34, 35n30, 38–39, 42, 65–66, 67, 69, 72, 74, 74–75, 78, 87, 91, 105, 109, 126; patent, 43; property, 2, 20, 26, 28, 29, 40, 52, 69

Roman Empire, 124
Rome, 88, 122
Rosarno, 83
Rouen, 123
Russia, 64

Said, Edward, 54, 55, 61, 67, 112; *Covering Islam: How the Media and the Experts Determine How We See the Rest of the World*, 67
Sakai, Naomi, 25, 39, 48, 55
Samarkand, 123
San Francisco, 83
Santos, Bonaventura de Sousa, 26
Sanyal, Kalyan, 43
Sartre, Jean-Paul, 46
Scandinavia, 28
Schmitt, Carl, 30
Scotland, 28, 43
Scott, David, 24
Seikaly, Sherene, 34
self, 2, 47, 51, 51–52, 55, 68, 70, 91, 104, 107, 110; care of, 52
Sephardic community in Salonica, 123
settler colonial societies, 105
A Seventh Man, 1
Seville, 123
Shonibare, Yinka, 97
Sijilmāsa, 123
Sissiko, Abderrahmane, 98; *Bamako*, 98
slavery, 3, 5, 7, 20, 24, 28, 31, 41–43, 58, 63, 77, 83
Smith, Adam, 73
Somalia, 76
souths of the world, 6, 20, 34, 35n32, 37–38, 43–45, 51, 61–62, 66, 74, 75, 84, 86, 113; epistemology, 28–29, 31, 45, 56, 62, 96; 'southern question', 32, 43–44, 81n54
South Africa, 53, 106
Spivak, Gayatri Chakravorty, 50; *A Critique of Postcolonial Reason*, 50
Stoler, Laura Ann, 32–33
subaltern, 6, 20, 31, 44, 46–47, 50, 54, 56–57, 61, 63, 66, 73, 85, 96, 98, 101, 103, 105, 113, 119, 126
Syria, 5, 66, 67, 68, 126

Tahrir Square, 51, 66

Taksim Square, 51
tarab, 114
Taussig, Michael, 47
Tazzioli, Martina, 64
Teheran, 71
Tel Aviv, 88
Terranova, Tiziana, 41
Thatcher, Margaret, 2
Thompson, E.P., 43; *The Making of the English Working Class*, 43
Tijuana, 106
Timor Sea, 106
Todorov, Tzevtan, 5
Trouillot, Michel-Ralph, 101
Tunis, 51, 67, 71, 86
Tunisia, 69

UK Border Agency, 75, 77
United Irishmen, 109
United Nations Declaration on Human Rights, 75

United States, 2, 28, 64, 75, 105, 106

Visconti, Luchino, 43; *Rocco and His Brothers*, 43
Venice, 123
voodoo, 109

Walcott, Derek, 46, 48, 107, 108
Warburg, Aby, 111
Weizman, Eyal, 77, 104
Williams, Eric, 41; *Capitalism and Slavery*, 41
Wolfe Tone, 109
World Bank, 51, 64

Yimer, Dagmawi, 125; *Asmat*, 125

Zaatari, Akran, 85, 86
Zionism, 77